Wisdom

—for—

Women

WISDOM FOR WOMEN
by Bob and Amy Beasley
ISBN 1-885358-31-8
©2002 by Legacy Press, fourth printing
Legacy reorder #DB46403

Editor: Ron Durham
Cover Design: Stray Cat Studio, San Diego, CA

Published by:
Legacy Press
P.O. Box 26119
San Diego, CA 92196

WISDOM —for— WOMEN

by Bob & Amy Beasley

LEGACY PRESS
A Division of Rainbow Publishers

For our mothers…

Teal Archer
and
Frances Cook Beasley

…in the Name of our heavenly Father.

"…and do not forsake your mother's teaching."
Proverbs 6:20

Mission Statement

Our goal in *Wisdom for Women* is to provide Christian women with a resource they can use to grow more like Christ through the study of the Proverbs and by looking at the many positive and negative examples of men and women in the Scriptures.

CONTENTS

ABOUT THE AUTHORS

Bob Beasley

Bob was born in Nashville, Tennessee, but has spent the majority of his life in San Diego, California. A graduate of Claremont McKenna College, he served as an Army officer before beginning his career in the real estate industry. He began in the commercial brokerage business and later developed residential properties in California, Texas, and Florida. In 1981, he formed COMPS InfoSystems, a firm that publishes confirmed market data of commercial property sales throughout the major metropolitan areas of the U.S. Bob is still involved in that company's growth.

Since he was called to Christ, Bob has taught Bible studies in his church, spoken at retreats and conferences, and taught several businessmen's Bible studies. He is a graduate of Westminster Theological Seminary and has three adult daughters.

Amy Beasley

Amy was born and reared in Hartville, a small town in northeastern Ohio. She graduated with a music degree from Houghton College in New York and went on to graduate study in voice at the University of Southern California. But following a decision that the operatic stage was not where God wanted her to spend her life, and after a year abroad in Berlin, she returned to the U.S. to focus on fund raising for non-profit organizations.

Amy's background in non-profit development led her to the University of San Diego, where she spent seven years raising funds for the university. She is currently pursuing, on a full-time basis, a master of international business degree at USD.

Amy was raised in a Christian home and was called to Christ at the age of 13. Amy and Bob met in the choir at their church in San Diego and were married in 1993.

PREFACE

The Woman of Proverbs 31

"Who is this Proverbs 31 woman, and why is she so important? She seems so 'perfect' it's discouraging…could anyone ever do all the things she does?"

Those are honest questions, and frankly, we think a person would go nuts if she tried to copy the Proverbs 31 woman's life exactly. But we are not to imitate her activities. Rather, we are to imitate her character. She is a model woman who embodies the righteous characteristics of Christ. Because we are called to imitate Christ (1 Cor. 4:16-17; Eph. 5:1), we may use her example as a guide for the Christian life.

In much of today's society, one may hear that the church is restrictive of women—not in tune with modern times. But, as you will see, the woman of these verses isn't restricted. Quite the opposite, she's a vital, fulfilled, joyful, multi-dimensional woman. Her life has been defined by God, who has set her free in Christ Jesus to be the woman He intended her to be. Just like her, our study of and meditation upon the Word of God sets us free to live a life pleasing to God—the most wonderful life imaginable.

How To Use This Book

Wisdom for Women is organized into weekly studies. Following an introductory page in each chapter, there are six proverb studies, succeeded by a "Study Questions and Projects" page. Although a person may choose to study alone, we recommend that at least one other friend be invited to join in. Study one proverb per day privately, with its personal illustrations of Bible characters, and perhaps complete some of the questions and projects. Then, at the end of the week, have a regularly scheduled meeting with others—perhaps over coffee at the kitchen table—reviewing the proverbs, discipling each other, and sharing guidance in the issues of life. Proverbs 27:17 says, "As iron sharpens iron, so one [woman] sharpens another." We all have blind spots, but we don't all have the same blind spots. Each one can help the other.

Working Together

We've been asked how we were able to work together to produce a book like this. Some couples would find it an extremely difficult—if not impossible—task. We simply applied Ephesians 5:21, "Submit to one another out of reverence for Christ." To "submit to one another" means to trust and value the other's judgment, and to constantly give thanks to God for the partnership that He has created. Our marriage gives us much joy, as we work together toward the common goal of glorifying the Lord.

The Bible's Hard Candy

Our pastor, George Miladin, calls Proverbs the "hard candy" of the Bible. The verses are not meant to be chewed and swallowed rapidly, but rather to be turned over and over in the cheek. Their sweetness and wisdom should be allowed to glide slowly over the spiritual taste buds and savored, as we are given the Spirit's insight into how each verse is best applied to our lives. All we have attempted to do is to remove the wrapper from the candy. We hope that the pure sweetness of God's Word and the straight paths down which it will lead you will bring great joy to your life.

Bob and Amy Beasley, San Diego

Proverbs 31:10-31

The Woman of Noble Character

"A wife of noble character who can find? She is worth far more than rubies. Her husband has full confidence in her and lacks nothing of value. She brings him good, not harm, all the days of her life. She selects wool and flax and works with eager hands. She is like the merchant ships, bringing her food from afar. She gets up while it is still dark; she provides food for her family and portions for her servant girls.

"She considers a field and buys it; out of her earnings she plants a vineyard. She sets about her work vigorously; her arms are strong for her tasks. She sees that her trading is profitable, and her lamp does not go out at night. In her hand she holds the distaff and grasps the spindle with her fingers. She opens her arms to the poor and extends her hands to the needy. When it snows, she has no fear for her household; for all of them are clothed in scarlet. She makes coverings for her bed; she is clothed in fine linen and purple. Her husband is respected at the city gate, where he takes his seat among the elders of the land. She makes linen garments and sells them, and supplies the merchants with sashes.

"She is clothed with strength and dignity; she can laugh at the days to come. She speaks with wisdom, and faithful instruction is on her tongue. She watches over the affairs of her household and does not eat the bread of idleness. Her children arise and call her blessed; her husband also, and he praises her: 'Many women do noble things, but you surpass them all.' Charm is deceptive, and beauty is fleeting; but a woman who fears the Lord is to be praised. Give her the reward she has earned, and let her works bring her praise at the city gate."

- Proverbs 31:10 -
A wife of noble character who can find?
She is worth far more than rubies.

Chapter One

A Woman of Great Value

In this day when there is much confusion over women's roles —in the family, in the church, and in the workplace—it is essential to look at what God values in a woman. Proverbs says her worth is "far more than rubies." But from what source does her worth come?

Many women look solely to their husbands for self-worth. In the daily grind, it's easy for a woman to lose herself in her family, her work, and even her church activities. Conversely, a woman might rebel against her role and begin to think that women are better than men—perhaps women should even control men! Of course, it is not in God's design for anyone to achieve self-esteem from control of another.

The Bible makes it clear that a woman's worth comes from her Lord and Savior, Jesus Christ. She is precious to Him. He died for her. Christ is her eternal husband who lifts her to the heavens.

Out of the new heart Christ gives us flows the "noble character" referred to in this proverb. Our response to God's love is to prayerfully seek His wisdom—and then to put that wisdom into action. In that way we will best glorify Him.

Let Wisdom Be Your Wealth and Adornment

*Gold there is, and rubies in abundance, but lips that speak
knowledge are a rare jewel* (Prov. 20:15).

Gold is known for its beauty and luster, its permanence and
weight, and is valued for its scarcity. Rubies are precious stones of
rare beauty. Both gold and rubies are prized for their intrinsic value
and for their beauty in jewelry. It is in such precious materials as
gold and rubies that the world puts its trust and gives its honor.

But there is jewelry of far greater value, and it is much more
beautiful than mere gold or rubies: the lips that speak knowledge.
This is not the world's knowledge, but the divine knowledge of
God. We can't just dig up this knowledge like we might dig gold
and rubies out of the ground. Knowledge is a gift from God and
must be sought from Him and His Word, through His Spirit.

Isaiah 52:7 speaks of the beauty of "the feet of those who bring
good news, who proclaim peace . . . who proclaim salvation." How
much are feet and lips of beauty needed in this world today. Let
your trust and ultimate security rest in His knowledge, and then
let your lips be your precious adornment.

Scriptural Examples

Ruth. What uncommon beauty her lips brought forth as she
clung to her mother-in-law, Naomi, and said, "Where you go I will
go, and where you stay I will stay. Your people will be my people
and your God my God" (Ruth 1:16).

Solomon. Solomon could have asked God for gold and rubies,
but he asked for wisdom to tell right from wrong and to govern
God's people. Because of his request, the Lord also showered
Solomon with wealth and honor (1 Kings 3:5-13).

The merchant and the pearl. Jesus told of a merchant who sold
everything he had to buy a pearl. The pearl was the wisdom that
was the key to the kingdom. It was infinitely more valuable than
all his other possessions (Matt. 13:45-46).

Prayer of Application

Father, what a treasure is stored up for those who love You.
Give us wisdom to use our lips to tell others of it, to the end that
we might bring glory to You, wisdom's great source.

Find Wisdom's Invaluable Wealth

Blessed is the man who finds wisdom, the man who gains
understanding, for she is more profitable than silver and yields
better returns than gold. She is more precious than rubies;
nothing you desire can compare with her (**Prov.** 3:13-15).

Several years ago, God opened our spiritual eyes in rebirth so that we could gaze upon the incredible riches of His treasure house of wisdom. Now, years later, we look back and realize that we only saw a small portion of God's treasure then. As we have studied His Word, we have mined riches of incredible value.

Jesus spoke of a man who sold all that he had to buy a field that contained a hidden treasure, and likened it to the treasures of heaven (Matt. 13:44). Another parable told of a woman who mixed yeast into a large amount of flour until it leavened all the dough (Matt. 13:33). So it is with God's wisdom, which is found in the person of Jesus Christ (1 Cor. 1:24). His wisdom says that we are not to put our trust in treasures on this earth like silver and gold and rubies. Rather, we are to put our trust in God, and lay up for ourselves treasures in heaven (Matt. 6:19-21). Does this mean that earthly wealth is a bad thing? No, but we should fix our eyes only on the One who is able to supply all our needs.

Scriptural Examples

Esther. She broke the law of King Xerxes when she went into his presence unannounced. She stood to lose not only her position and treasure, but her very life. Nevertheless, she trusted God and followed in the wisdom of her cousin Mordecai (Est. 4:12–5:2).

The idolators. God said their treasures were worthless. There is but one Rock. All other "rocks" like rubies and precious metals are nothing compared to Him (Isa. 44:8-9).

The rich young man. Jesus saw through his coveteousness and the young man went away sorrowfully. Heavenly riches eluded the man because of his idolatry (Matt. 19:16-22).

Prayer of Application

Heavenly Father, thank You for allowing me to see Your riches in Christ Jesus. Help me to mine those riches wisely, to the end that I would glorify You and receive a rich eternal inheritance.

Seek the Inner Beauty of Wisdom

Like a gold ring in a pig's snout is a beautiful woman who shows no discretion (Prov. 11:22).

We were both raised near farmland; Bob in Tennessee and Amy in Ohio. We've both seen pigs in their sties and remember as children how we always kept a safe distance as those squealing animals rooted around in the mud and the slop looking for choice morsels to eat. It's hard to imagine one of those porkers with an expensive gold ring in its nose. Why would God use such a hideous example to describe a beautiful woman who is devoid of wisdom? Perhaps it's because that's exactly how He sees her.

The swine is doubly horrible as an example because it was held in scorn by the people of Israel, since the Law of Moses forbade them to eat it (Lev. 11:7). The gold ring in a pig's flat snout only mocks the reality of who a woman really is. Charles Bridges put it this way in *Proverbs*, p. 123: "Many a lovely form enshrines a revolting mind." To have external beauty without its corresponding inner quality is a mockery.

Scriptural Examples

Ruth. Unfortunately, Ruth lived before oil paintings or cameras were invented, so we don't know what she looked like. Bob is sure that she was a rare beauty. But Ruth's true beauty resided in her heart as a woman of loyalty and character (Ruth 2:11-12).

Abigail. The wife of the foolish Nabal was blessed by David for her discretion and wisdom. Her quick thinking in bringing food to David and his men following her husband's scorn of them kept David from vengeance (1 Sam. 25:33).

Michal. Saul's beautiful daughter and David must have had a stormy relationship. One day David danced openly before the Lord. Michal chided him for what she considered a vulgar display unfit for a king, and "despised him in her heart." God made Michal barren the rest of her days (2 Sam. 6:16-23).

Prayer of Application

Dear Father, keep me from putting too much emphasis upon physical appearance. Rather may I value the true inner beauty that only Your Spirit gives to both women and men.

Beware of Praising Yourself

Better to be a nobody and yet have a servant than pretend to be somebody and have no food (Prov. 12:9).

Growing up in the South, Bob heard many Civil War era stories about fabulously wealthy plantation owners. Following the war, many of these families were virtually penniless, yet they tried to maintain appearances of wealth. Humbled by God and the Northern forces, they refused to be humbled in their own minds. What foolish vanity! But many in America do exactly this today. They mortgage themselves to the hilt to impress others with their possessions, then hardly have enough money left after all their payments to buy food.

To seek praise and honor for one's own self is always foolishness because it impresses no one. But how much more foolish to promote one's own honor when there's nothing to honor. Such is the plight of anyone who finds herself a slave to the opinions of others. A "nobody" with meager personal possessions is better off than the proud boaster who doesn't even know from whence her next meal is coming.

Scriptural Examples

Mephibosheth. This grandson of King Saul was left destitute, humbled by a crippling childhood injury. David sought to honor him and to return to him all of the land his grandfather Saul had owned. Mephibosheth humbly bowed down to David and called himself a "dead dog" (2 Sam. 9:6-8).

Jezebel. This foolish queen was proud and boastful. When her sappy husband, Ahab, sulked because he couldn't get Naboth's vineyard, she boldly suggested a wicked, deadly plan (1 Kings 21).

The wedding guests. Jesus said that if you go to a wedding feast, take the lowest seat. The host may ask you to take a more elevated place. But if you take the best seat, he may ask that you give it up to a more highly honored guest (Luke 14:8-11).

Prayer of Application

Lord, grant that the same mind which was in Christ Jesus be also in me. He made Himself of no reputation, but humbled Himself, that He might accomplish our salvation.

Desire a Good Name from God and Others

A good name is more desirable than great riches; to be esteemed is better than silver or gold (Prov. 22:1).

Riches are nothing to sneeze at, particularly when they are used for God's kingdom. But even great riches are surpassed by a good name. To have great riches and a bad name may mean that one acquired her wealth by devious or selfish means. Such wealth is worthless (Prov. 11:4). Likewise, to have a good name before others but not before God is a hollow sham. A good name in God's sight is infinitely more valuable. However, to think that you can obtain a good name before God without a good name before others is to be self-righteous. There should be no tension between how we walk before God and how we walk before our neighbors.

To be esteemed by both God and others is true riches. But the greatest wealth imaginable is to have your "good name" written in God's Book of Life (Rev. 20:15; Ps. 69:28). It is a good name only by the grace of God, and for those whose names are listed there it is a reason for great joy—much greater joy than mere earthly power or wealth could ever bring (Luke 10:20).

Scriptural Examples

Mrs. Lot. She's the woman who looked back at Sodom and became a pillar of salt. She probably missed the world's riches, and thus missed out on the riches of God (Gen. 19:26).

Job. This wealthy man was blessed with a good name before God. God said that His servant Job was a blameless and upright man who feared God and shunned evil (Job 1:8).

Mary. What a wonderful name! Filled with the Holy Spirit, Elizabeth exclaimed of her, "Blessed are you among women!" (Luke 1:42).

Cornelius. This Gentile centurion had a good name with the Jews who knew him. He loved the Hebrew nation and even built a synagogue for them (Luke 7:4-5).

Prayer of Application

Father, help me to live my life seeking a good name from You alone. The result of a life that is pleasing to You will also produce a good name in the sight of others.

Know the Perfect Word of God

*Does not wisdom call out? Does not understanding raise her voice?
On the heights along the way, where the paths meet, she takes her
stand; beside the gates leading into the city, at the entrances, she
cries aloud: "To you, O men, I call out; I raise my voice to all
mankind. You who are simple, gain prudence; you who are
foolish, gain understanding. Listen, for I have worthy things to say;
I open my lips to speak what is right. My mouth speaks what is
true, for my lips detest wickedness. All the words of my mouth are
just; none of them is crooked or perverse. To the discerning all of
them are right; they are faultless to those who have knowledge.
Choose my instruction instead of silver, knowledge rather than
choice gold, for wisdom is more precious than rubies, and nothing
you desire can compare with her"* (Prov. 8:1-11).

Godly wisdom is found in the perfect Word of God: the Bible.
The Bible stands at the crossroads of life (v. 2b) and cries out to all
people (v. 4b): "Open me, read me, study me, love me. Because in
me you will find what is right and true and just. My words are
without fault or error, and for the one who truly seeks, they are easy
to understand. They are more valuable than any other treasure.
Nothing can compare to the riches of the Word of God" (Prov.
8:4-11, authors' paraphrase).

For us, all theology may be rendered down to this verse of a
child's hymn: "Jesus loves me, this I know, for the Bible tells me
so." Know the Word of God. Read it, study it, trust it, and above
all, obey it. In it is God's perfect wisdom.

Scriptural Examples

Paul. He knew and lived the Word of God. He was also used
by God to write down His truth for all generations. Follow Paul,
as he followed Christ in believing and obeying the very Word of
God (1 Tim. 3:4-17; John 10:35; 17:17; Phil. 2:8).

Prayer of Application

Dear Father, thank You for Your Word and for the Holy Spirit
who guides me into its depths. Your Word is truth. I pray that
through it I will be fully equipped for every good work.

Study Questions and Projects

1) Read 1 Peter 3:3-4.
   a) What does Peter say is highly prized in God's sight?
   b) What isn't necessarily prized at all?

2) In Jeremiah 1:5, when does God say He knew the prophet? (See also Ps. 139.) In light of Romans 8:29-30, how do you think God's statement to Jeremiah (or in the Psalms) applies to you? What value do these texts place upon you as a person and child of God? Discuss with others.

3) John 8:1-11 tells the story of Jesus and the woman accused of adultery. How do you think the focus of her life changed after this encounter with Christ? How do you think her understanding of self-worth changed? How is a sinful pattern in one's life connected to self-worth? Discuss with others.

4) In the midst of Job's suffering, his wife spoke out (Job 2:9). What did she say? How does her statement and attitude measure up to the verses in 1 Peter?

5) Read Isaiah 66:1-2. What two characteristics does God esteem? What basis does God give in these verses for the legitimacy of His rule over us?

6) Esther 10:3 gives two reasons why Mordecai was held in high regard among his people. What are they? In what ways are you doing likewise today? What more could you do?

Other Verses to Study
Proverbs 4:8; Isaiah 32:9-20; Romans 16:19.

One to Memorize
A good name is more desirable than great riches; to be esteemed is better than silver or gold (Prov. 22:1).

My Personal Action Plan to Be a Woman of Great Value

1) _____ 2) _____

3) _____ 4)_____

- Proverbs 31:11 -
Her husband has full confidence in her
and lacks nothing of value.

Chapter Two

A Woman Who Is Trusted

How wonderful it is to have the full trust and confidence of your husband, your family, your friends, and your work associates! As we all know from experience, trust is something that must be earned. It must be carefully built and nurtured, and it can be easily destroyed. "Don't you trust me?" is the teenager's perennial cry. The usual parental response is, " I'll trust you as soon as you prove to me that you *can* be trusted."

How do we build the confidence and trust of others? We do it through many small, consistent actions that reflect our walk with Jesus Christ. Just as a teenager must demonstrate maturity to gain the rewards and challenges of greater responsibility, so we too must earn the trust of others.

This is especially true of the relationship between husband and wife. In the authors' marriage, we allow each other a lot of freedom. Each of us appreciates the balance of time together and time apart. Our overriding attitude is one of trust. But this cannot be taken lightly. It would take only one sinful act to damage the trust we've built, so we guard our relationship preciously. Praise God that He has given all those who love Him the desire *and* the ability to become men and women who can be trusted.

Wives, Honor Your Husbands

A wife of noble character is her husband's crown, but a disgraceful wife is like decay in his bones (Prov. 12:4).

What a great gap divides the two women of this verse. The disgraceful wife seeks her own honor. She provokes arguments. She cares only about what her husband can do for her. Her love is contingent upon his performance. Her eyes may wander to other men. She may be sloppy in her administration of the family. But her main problem is that she has no interest in the things of God. The love of God is not in her (Prov. 31:30).

The virtuous woman is faithful to her husband (Prov. 31:11-12). She is pure (Titus 2:5). She delights in being under her husband's care and teaching (Eph. 5:25-27). She loves her husband and seeks his highest good. She is affectionate to both him and her children (Titus 2:4). She manages her household carefully. (Prov. 14:11). She is considerate of others and kind to the poor. (Prov. 31: 20, 26b). Finally, and most importantly, she reverences the name of the Lord God (Prov. 31:30). Future wives, remember that the man of God will look for the last quality first—a woman who reveres and follows Christ. Practice it!

Scriptural Examples

Eve. Eve was created by God as a helper for her husband, Adam (Gen. 2:18). But Satan made her into Adam's temptress. She was tempted by pride and led astray by her own appetites. She gave some of the fruit to her husband (Gen. 3:1-6).

Ruth. This fine and virtuous Moabitess became a crown to her husband, Boaz. He became her kinsman-redeemer. The book of Ruth is a picture of Christ and His church, a bride for the Lamb (the book of Ruth and Rev. 21:9-11).

Gomer. God told Hosea to go and take a vile and adulterous woman to be his wife. So he married Gomer. She is a picture of the adulterous nation Israel (the book of Hosea).

Prayer of Application

Father, encourage and strengthen me as I seek to honor Christ by obeying Your Word and bringing honor to my husband. May my devotion to You shine brightly in today's lost world.

Let Your Words Spring from Wisdom's Waters

The words of a man's mouth are deep waters, but the fountain of wisdom is a bubbling brook (**Prov. 18:4**).

We have here the storehouse and the delivery of wisdom. As we mature in Christ, we store up the wisdom of God (Ps. 119:11). It becomes a deep reservoir of truth and "uncommon" sense, ready to spring forth for the benefit of others.

The words we speak reveal our heart. If it is filled with pollution, foolish words will gush out. If filled with the truth of God's Word, our words will be a well-spring of wisdom, bringing up life and truth and causing our hearers to trust us.

First, our words will honor God, bringing glory to His name. They will point the way to His salvation and edify our brothers and sisters. Second, our words will heal, bringing justice, unity, and peace to our neighbors. Third, our words will provide loving guidance and encouragement for others.

Pray that your words will be as a crystal-clear mountain spring, welling up from a deep reservoir of the heart. Pray that as others trust your words, they will see Christ in you.

Scriptural Examples

Jethro. Moses' father-in-law saw that Moses' role as judge was too weighty, so he offered wisdom out of the depths of his understanding. He advised Moses to appoint capable men to assist him in the task. Moses trusted his advice (Ex. 18:11-24).

Solomon. The queen of Sheba came to visit, bringing with her some tough questions to test Solomon's wisdom. She was amazed at the depth of the wisdom she found (1 Kings 10:1-7).

Gamaliel. This Pharisee stood up in front of the Sanhedrin and wisely addressed them regarding the persecution of Christians. He said that if this new sect was of God, there was nothing they could do to stop it. We don't know whether Gamaliel ever became a believer, but he spoke with godly wisdom (Acts 5:33-40).

Prayer of Application

Father God, how Your wisdom thrills my heart and satisfies my soul. Create in me a deep reservoir of Your love and truth, and let the words of my mouth cause others to trust my words.

Nip Strife in the Bud

Starting a quarrel is like breaching a dam; so drop the matter before a dispute breaks out (**Prov.** 17:14).

We think of the young man in Holland with his finger in a dike that had sprung a leak. His finger, in effect, was keeping the entire North Atlantic out of the fields of his homeland. Were a small hole to be left unattended, it would increasingly widen until the whole dike was breached, and the land was flooded.

The proper time to correct a relational problem is at the beginning of the problem. The longer it is allowed to fester, the more serious it becomes. Trust disappears. Someone has said that we should "keep short accounts." This is particularly important in marriage. We should not let the sun go down on our anger (Eph. 4:26). To the good advice to "kiss and make up" should be added this: "And do it quickly." It builds trust.

Scriptural Examples

Israel and Sihon. Israel sent an envoy to the Amorites, seeking passage through their country. Sihon, the Amorite king, refused and attacked the Israelites, only to be soundly defeated. He could have saved himself much trouble and anguish by simply fulfilling their request (Num. 21:21-24).

The disciples and Jesus. The disciples had been arguing about who would be greatest among them. Jesus settled the argument quickly by telling them that whoever wanted to be first among them must be the servant of all (Mark 9:33-35).

Paul and Barnabas. These great men argued about taking Mark with them on a journey. Ultimately peace was restored, even though it meant parting company (Acts 15:36-40).

Euodia and Syntyche. Paul mentions these women in Philippians 4:2 and pleads with them to agree with one another. We don't know what the trouble was, but we do know that Paul used godly wisdom, as we are suggesting.

Prayer of Application

Help me, Lord, to solve my relational problems with others quickly, and before they get too large and out of control. May my desire for fellowship restore trust to the relationship.

Bless Your Children by Your Faithful Walk

The righteous man leads a blameless life; blessed are
his children after him (Prov. 20:7).

Who you are speaks so loudly to your children, and to others, they often can't hear what you say. If you talk a good game, but don't walk in a manner that conforms to it, you are not practicing integrity. Integrity comes when one lives what she says she believes.

There is a very foolish belief in some evangelical circles today that since we are no longer "under law, but under grace" (Rom. 6:14), the Christian can do anything he or she pleases and be accepted by God. This is absolute nonsense. While grace is vulnerable to this kind of irresponsible presumption, it never teaches it. We are "under grace" inasmuch as we are able to choose right over wrong or integrity rather than hypocrisy. By God's grace, and the indwelling presence of the Holy Spirit, we are no longer slaves to sin, but rather slaves to righteousness (Rom. 6:16-19). Christ has called us to lead a blameless life.

The mother who has been called of God will want to walk in integrity. If she doesn't, her children will see through the ruse quickly, and the trust between them will vanish.

Scriptural Examples

Naomi. Following her husband, Elimelech, into Moab, she witnessed his death and that of her two sons, Mahlon and Kilion. But Ruth, the daughter she gained, was to be richly blessed by her mother-in-law's faithful walk (Ruth 1).

Hannah. This faithful woman prayed fervently that God would give her a son. When Samuel was born, she dedicated him to the Lord, and after he was weaned, she took him to live with Eli. Samuel became a great prophet of God (1 Sam. 1:9-28).

Lois and Eunice. These women blessed Timothy by their faithful walk, and in turn, have blessed all Christians through the centuries, their "children in Christ" (2 Tim. 1:5).

Prayer of Application

Heavenly Father, keep me in the way of righteousness by Your mighty hand. May my children see the evidence of Your hand upon me and be blessed, giving You the glory.

Trust in God Alone

Trust in the Lord with all your heart and lean not on your own understanding; in all your ways acknowledge him, and he will make your paths straight (Prov. 3:5-6).

Many of us list these verses as some of our favorites. But do we really understand what they are saying to us?

First, we are to trust the Sovereign Lord with every fiber of our being, putting the full weight of our cares, worries, and problems on Him (1 Peter 5:7; Matt. 11:28-30). We are to place our trust solely in God Almighty and His Word (Job 13:15a). This is easy to say, but very difficult to do. It runs counter to our sin nature and upbringing. Many are raised to be self-reliant, but self-reliance is condemned by God (Prov. 28:26). Self-reliance is the province of the fool, not the wise man. Self-reliance is idolatry.

How can we trust Him fully? Verse 6 shows us the way. The word "acknowledge" is better rendered as "know" (Kidner, *Proverbs*, p. 63). To "know" God is to have intimate fellowship with Him. We are to prayerfully and consistently study and ingest His Word (2 Tim. 2:15), growing daily in our knowledge of Him (2 Peter 3:18). The more we truly *know* Him, the more we will trust in Him, and less in ourselves and others.

We who have trusted God for our salvation and our eternal security, how can we not therefore trust Him for all things? (Rom. 8:32.) Let us then get up on our feet and run the straight path set out before us, trusting only in Jesus, who is the author and the perfector of our faith (Heb. 12:1-2).

Scriptural Examples

Daniel. Daniel's trust lay fully in his God. Three times a day he would prayerfully seek God's face for help and sustenance. Wicked men tried to use his faith against him, but even in the den of lions God had Daniel on a straight path. Later, his enemies and their entire families found themselves on the menu (Dan. 6:11-24).

Prayer of Application

Dear Lord, help me to grasp the truth of these verses in its full meaning and power, to the end that I would trust You fully in every area of my life. Help me to know You more each day.

Treasure Lasting Friendships

Do not forsake your friend and the friend of your father, and do not go to your brother's house when disaster strikes you—better a neighbor nearby than a brother far away (Prov. 27:10).

God intends the church to be a place of service, not entertainment. We should decide upon a church home and then stick with it (Prov. 27:8). This proverb gives us a further reason. We need to send down roots of friendship. First, so we will have, and *be*, trusted advisors and counselors (Prov. 27:9). Second, God wants us to have a solid underpinning of support when trouble or disaster strikes. That support network is not just for ourselves, but for our children and their children, too.

Amy's family lives 3,000 miles away. While we can pick up the phone and talk to them for counsel and encouragement, we simply can't depend on them for physical help if one of us falls down the stairs and breaks a leg. We need friends close by on whom we can call in times of physical need. What better place to find that circle of friends than in our church home? A single phone call can start a prayer chain, or bring rapid help. Invest time and energy into friendships. They are a rare treasure.

Scriptural Examples

Solomon and Hiram. When Solomon succeeded David on the throne, Hiram, King of Tyre, sent an envoy to him. Hiram wanted his friendship with David to carry over to his son. Solomon sent back word of his decision to build a temple for the glory of God. Would Hiram supply the cedar for it? You bet Hiram would! He supplied all the wood Solomon needed (1 Kings 5:1-10).

Rehoboam and the elders. It's a pity that Solomon's son didn't have his father's wisdom. When Rehoboam became king, he sought the advice of Solomon's friends and advisors, but then rejected it in favor of the advice of his young and foolish cronies, to his ultimate regret (1 Kings 12:6-19).

Prayer of Application

Dear God, thank You again for the church home to which You have called me, and for the many friends who would stop whatever they are doing to come to my aid if I am in need.

Study Questions and Projects

1) Hebrews 3:7–4:11 tells of God's anger against the Hebrews. What had they done to provoke such vehemence from their Lord? What punishment did God inflict?

a) Deuteronomy 9:23 gives two succinct reasons why it all occurred. What are they? Where do you stand in relation to these points?

b) Have you ever experienced someone's lack of trust? Was it deserved? Was it not deserved? How did it make you feel? What did you do about it? Share your experiences with others in the group.

2) Read Esther 1:10-12. What do you think Queen Vashti was thinking? What did she hope to accomplish? What *did* she accomplish?

3) Read Esther 5:1-5. The new queen makes a request of Xerxes. How does his response differ from that of Vashti's to the same request? How is the element of trust (or distrust) displayed in these examples? Discuss with others.

4) Read 1 Samuel 25. What lessons do you think God wanted to teach us about relationships from this story of Nabal and Abigail? Do you think she trusted her husband? Why or why not? Did she trust David? Why or why not? Discuss.

Other Verses to Study
Psalm 37:4-6; Proverbs 3:5-6; Nehemiah 1:7; Romans 15:13.

One to Memorize
A wife of noble character is her husband's crown,
but a disgraceful wife is like decay in his bones (Prov. 12:4).

My Personal Action Plan to Be a
Woman Who Is Trusted

1) _____ 2) _____

3) _____ 4) _____

- Proverbs 31:12 -
*She brings him good, not harm,
all the days of her life.*

Chapter Three

A Woman Who Loves
●●●●●●●●●●●●●●●●●●●●●●●●●●●●●

Amy's favorite holiday is Valentine's Day. Although Bob knows this (and responds appropriately), the strong relationship we've built is based on much more than candy and flowers on one day of the year. Our love flows from a common respect and the desire to bring the other "good, not harm." Our lives are tied up in one another, and we must love each other even as we love ourselves.

A Christian woman has been given a supernatural love from God. God's love, described by Paul in 1 Corinthians 13, is a love that transcends all emotion or human reason. Only through Christ can we love others as God intended.

Putting love into action is the hardest part, and is made possible only by the Holy Spirit. Love seeks peace among brothers and sisters. Listen to Paul's words: "Love is patient, love is kind. It does not envy, it does not boast, it is not proud. It is not rude, it is not self-seeking, it is not easily angered, it keeps no record of wrongs. Love does not delight in evil but rejoices with the truth. It always protects, always trusts, always hopes, always perserveres. Love never fails." That's a lot of ground for love to cover, as these proverbs will attest.

Build Your Home in the Love of Christ

The wise woman builds her house, but with her own hands the foolish one tears hers down (**Prov. 14:1**).

A wise wife and mother blesses her family. She will order her household with diligence, and raise up her children in loving discipline, and in the wisdom of Christ and His Word.

The foolish woman, on the other hand, tears down her house, even though she may do it inadvertently. She may be given to idleness, waste, and love of pleasure. She may neglect the spiritual and even the physical needs of her children, not disciplining them. She may be contentious toward her husband, failing to submit to his leadership, as unto Christ (Eph. 5:22). Without Christ, she may have the appearance of a model wife and mother, but she is doomed to ultimate failure.

The impact of a wife and mother upon her family is crucial and beyond measure. Sometimes it's the little decisions we make, and the words we say, that can either tear down or build up our families. Devote yourself to God, and to His Word, and build up your family in His love.

Scriptural Examples

Jezebel. Ahab, king of Israel, married this woman outside the nation of Israel in direct defiance of God. The wicked king reaped the bitter fruit of his rebellion (1 Kings 16:31; 21:25).

Hannah. Hannah prayed for her son, Samuel, and gave him up fully to the work of the Lord. God, throughout Scripture, honors women who honor Him (1 Sam. 1:27-28).

The wife and mother of Proverbs 31. Here is a wonderful picture of a godly wife and mother. She earned the respect and admiration of all in her community (Prov. 31:10-31).

Eunice. Paul told us of the faithfulness of Timothy's mother, and his grandmother Lois, to raise her boy in the nurture and admonition of the Lord (2 Tim. 1:5; 3:15).

Prayer of Application

Lord, make me the person that You want me to be, through the sanctification of washing by the Word. Help me to love, respect, and support those in my family, dying daily for them.

Seek Harmony in Your Families

He who brings trouble on his family will inherit only wind, and the fool will be servant to the wise (Prov. 11:29).

To cause division in the home or in the church is to inherit the wind of the fool, and not the blessings of the wise. The common denominator of unity is love, while that of division is sin. Sin always causes division as surely as the love that Jesus teaches us brings peace and harmony.

A short time ago in San Diego, a young police officer was shot to death while responding to a domestic violence situation. Violence in families is now a common occurrence throughout America and can be directly attributed to sin. Drug and alcohol abuse, adultery, contentiousness, and slothfulness are just a few of the sins that torment the American home.

The Christian family, both in the home and in the church body, is to be a place of peace, rest, and sanctity. Harmony is to be protected and encouraged. Selfishness, pride, gossip, envy, covetousness, and the like are great dividing principles. Love, joy, longsuffering, gentleness, kindness, and the other fruits of the Spirit are the principles of peace (Gal. 5:19–6:2).

Scriptural Examples

Miriam. Moses' sister was a fine woman who was faithful to him—at least most of the time. In one instance, however, she almost split the family apart with her contentiousness. God did not let her get away with it (Num. 12:1-10).

Pilate's wife. She probably didn't interfere in matters of state often, but in the matter of the Nazarene who had been brought up before Pilate by the Jews, she lovingly warned her husband of her dream (Matt. 27:19).

Mary and Martha. These sisters loved Jesus and loved each other. But there was a time when a dispute arose between them. Jesus quickly calmed the situation (Luke 10:38-42).

Prayer of Application

Merciful heavenly Father, may I manifest the fruit of Your Spirit of love as I seek to live out my life in Christ, to the end that there would be unity in my home, and in the body of believers.

Prefer Poverty and Peace to Treasure and Trouble

Better a little with the fear of the Lord than great wealth with turmoil. Better a meal of vegetables where there is love than a fattened calf with hatred (**Prov. 15:16-17**).

Have you seen the bumper sticker, "He who dies with the most toys wins"? This slogan says that success comes from the accumulation of stuff. But Jesus said that a person's life does not consist in the abundance of her possessions (Luke 12:15). All of the treasure in this world will not satisfy a worldly appetite (Eccl. 1:8), yet a very small portion of this world's goods will satisfy a person who fears the Lord. Paul says that "godliness with contentment is great gain"(1 Tim. 6:6).

Notice that the sources of the cheerful heart of verse 15 are the fear of the Lord (verse 16) and love for others (verse 17). For the person who has these attributes by the Spirit of God, life should be a continuing feast, regardless of her external circumstances.

On the other hand, in a house filled with great treasure, yet where sin abounds, there is trouble. There may be a superficial peace, but underneath that façade is rebellion against God that can only mean big trouble in an ultimate sense.

Scriptural Examples

Saul. David was invited to come to King Saul's feast, but no love was there. Saul in anger and jealousy even hurled his spear at his own son Jonathan (1 Sam. 20:24-34).

Tamar. David's daughter was lured into Amnon's bedroom and raped. Her brother Absalom later took revenge. David's household had great trouble as well as riches (2 Sam 13:28-29).

Jesus. The disciples enjoyed a simple meal of fish. It wasn't fancy cooking in a palace, but with the risen Lord and His love, it was a joyful feast (John 21:10-14).

The apostles. The new church led by these men met joyfully in homes to share their simple food (Acts 2:46).

Prayer of Application

Father, help me to fix my eyes on the true riches of holy reverence for You, love for others, and the peace that passes all understanding. Thank You for the many blessings You bring.

Seek Peace in All of Your Relationships

Hatred stirs up dissension, but love covers over all wrongs
(Prov. 10:12).

Another way to state this proverb is: "Sin separates; love unifies." Sin separates us from intimate fellowship with both God and our fellow man. Love reunites in its perfect bond.

In a parallel verse in 1 Peter 4:8, we read that "love covers over a multitude of sins." Does this mean that love hides sin? No. While love never gossips about the sin of another, there are times when love sheds light on sin. In such cases, our goal is to be reunited with our sinning brother or sister (Matt. 18:15).

Our local church should be a model of unity. But we often hear of a congregation torn apart by divisiveness. God hates this (Prov. 6:19). Does this mean that we should allow essential doctrine to be polluted in the interests of unity? Never. Rather, we are to consider our brother or sister first, submitting to one another in love out of reverence for Christ (Eph. 5:21).

Scriptural Examples

Satan. Why did Satan seek to cause dissension between Adam, Eve, and God? Satan hated all three and opposed the purposes of God. By his hatred and lies, Satan stirred up dissension where there had been unity (Gen. 3:1-6).

The Creator. When Adam and Eve sinned, their bond of intimacy slipped away. Their nakedness became apparent, and they covered themselves with fig leaves. But God, in His love for them, covered Adam and Eve with the skins of animals, slain in anticipation of the One who would be slain for their salvation and eternal unity with Him (Gen. 3:7, 21).

The Corinthians. There were dissensions in this church caused by petty jealousy and bickering. As he wrote in Colossians 3:14, Paul urges us all to put on the love that binds us together in perfect unity (1 Cor. 1:10-13).

Prayer of Application

Father God, help me to be a true minister of reconciliation. In my congregation of believers, help me to be a part of the glue that binds us all together in the love of our wonderful Savior.

Open Wide the Gates of Love

He who loves a quarrel loves sin; he who builds a high gate invites destruction (**Prov. 17:19**).

If you are like us, you hate to argue and will do almost anything to avoid conflict, unless your principles and convictions are being compromised. But we have both known people who love to quarrel. They seem to flourish in strife, because they love it. These are the people of whom this proverb speaks.

These lovers of strife have as their basic problem the sin of pride (Prov. 13:10). They "build a high gate" between themselves and those around them. Their superiority demands that everyone else see things their way, even though it may not be backed with the authority of Scripture. They are self-willed, not God-willed, and rarely resist any opportunity for conflict.

The Bible is very clear in condemning the sin of pride and its fruits of hatred, discord, dissensions, factions, and the like. Paul says that people who live like that will not inherit the kingdom of God (Gal. 5:19-21). As the apostle Paul instructs in Romans 12:18, "If it is possible, as far as it depends on you, live at peace with everyone." Open wide the gates of love.

Scriptural Examples

Gerar's herdsmen. These men quarrelled with the herdsmen of Isaac over water rights. They were Philistines who seemed to love to fight, particularly with the people of God. Humbly, Isaac's herdsmen sought other wells (Gen. 26:20-22).

The Benjamites. Benjamites from Gibeah raped a visitor's concubine, who subsequently died. The Ephraimite cut her body into twelve pieces, sending one to each tribe of Israel. The men of Israel rose up against their brothers in the tribe of Benjamin who had "built a high gate" and refused to bring the wicked perpetrators to justice. Virtually the entire tribe of Benjamin was annihilated at the hands of its brothers (Judg. 19:22–21:25).

Prayer of Application

Lord, help me to overlook the small things that can add fuel to an argument. But give me the strength to confront the person who sins against me, in a spirit of love and restoration.

Overlook Small Offenses

*He who covers over an offense promotes love, but whoever repeats
the matter separates close friends* (**Prov. 17:9**).

Jesus' primary role on this earth was to show forth the love of
God. He exhibited that love in His perfect life and ultimately in
dying for lost sinners. He provided a covering for our sins against
God. Jesus doesn't overlook sins (1 Pet. 4:8), but we are called to
overlook small offenses against us.

But what about major offenses? Suppose a sister sins against
you. You are to humbly go to your sister and tell her of the matter
(Matt. 18:15). If she seeks forgiveness, you are obliged to forgive
her, up to an innumerable number of times (Matt. 18:22). This
should restore an atmosphere of love between children of God.

The absolutely wrong thing to do is to go and tell others about
your sister's sin, without first seeking her out. If she does not ask
for forgiveness, you are to go to her a second time, this time with
two or three witnesses. If she still won't listen, then bring the
matter up before the church at large. If, after all of this, she still will
not listen, the elders are to expel her from church membership
(Matt. 18:16-17). Church disciplinary procedures are not to punish the sinning brother or sister. Rather, they serve to urge him or
her to repent and be reconciled to fellowship.

Scriptural Examples

David and Mephibosheth. David, in spite of the injustices
rendered to him by Saul, desired to show kindness to the house of
Saul for Jonathan's sake. David befriended the crippled
Mephibosheth, took him into his palace, and restored all of his
grandfather's land to him (2 Sam. 9).

Ziba and Mephibosheth. Ziba slandered Mephibosheth, the
invalid son of King Saul, by telling David that he was awaiting
ascension to Saul's throne. This deceit damaged the friendship of
David and Mephibosheth (2 Sam. 16:3-4).

Prayer of Application

Heavenly Father, help me to reflect the love of Christ in all of
my relationships with others. Help me to overlook small offenses,
as I hope others will overlook mine against them.

Study Questions and Projects

1) Read 1 Corinthians 13. Conduct an honest self-inventory on godly love. Next to each aspect of *agape* love, comment on how you view your life with regard to that aspect. Compare your list with others'. Pray for each other and use the action plan below to take needed steps. Use another sheet of paper if necessary.

- a) Patience: _____
- b) Kindness: _____
- c) Envy: _____
- d) Boastfulness: _____
- e) Pride: _____
- f) Rudeness: _____
- g) Self-seeking: _____
- h) Temper/Anger: _____
- i) Forgiveness: _____
- j) Gossip: _____
- k) Truthfulness: _____
- l) Protectiveness: _____
- m) Trustfulness:_____
- n) Hopefulness:_____
- o) Perserverance: _____

Other Verses to Study
Leviticus 19:18; Proverbs 15:17; Matthew 19:19; John 13:34-35.

One to Memorize
Hatred stirs up dissension,
but love covers over all wrongs (Prov. 10:12).

My Personal Action Plan to Be a
Woman Who Loves

1) _____ 2) _____

3) _____ 4) _____

- Proverbs 31:13 -
*She selects wool and flax
and works with eager hands.*

Chapter Four

A Woman of Industry
•••••••••••••••••••••••••••

God's command to honor the Sabbath day in Exodus 20:8-11 also has this command in verse 9: "Six days you shall labor and do all your work." Many think that work is a curse God put upon mankind because of the Fall. But a careful reading of the first chapters of Genesis reveals that this is not so. God gave Adam and his helpmate, Eve, *meaningful* work to do. They were to be rulers (Gen. 1:26), gardeners (2:15), and the first scientific team (2:19-20), as they classified the creatures that God had made and put on the earth. Adam's sin brought frustration—thorns and thistles—to work (Gen. 3:18).

Our God is a worker, and we are called to be like Him (Lev. 11:44-45). Jesus said in John 5:17, "My Father is always at his work to this very day, and I, too, am working." Work is part of God's blessing to us; not His curse. Whether we work in the home, in an office or factory, or in the church, our work can be a real joy if we will take the right perspective of it. Paul said in Colossians 3:23-24, "Whatever you do, work at it with all your heart, as working for the Lord, not for men, since you know that you will receive an inheritance from the Lord as a reward. It is the Lord Christ you are serving." If you take that perspective, frustration disappears! You report directly to the God of all creation—it is He who signs your paycheck.

Rise and Shine

Do not love sleep or you will grow poor; stay awake and you will have food to spare (Prov. 20:13).

"Rise and shine" were our mothers' words as each made the rounds, getting us sleepyheaded kids out of the sack. It was a tough job. That bed was so warm and cozy! How we longed for just a few more minutes to roll over and drift back to sleep. But a day stood waiting to be conquered, and every moment lost was a moment never to be regained. So, "Rise and shine," they cried.

It's a blessing that both of us have become "morning people." While not essential for marital bliss, it certainly makes life a lot easier. Bob still gets to the coffeepot first, while Amy is a close second. But we confess to being guilty of another form of sleepfulness, which also can lead to a kind of poverty—spiritual drowsiness. We can be sleepyheads on matters of discernment. Our eyelids often close when we should be watchful in prayer (Matt. 26:40). We need to awake to the "rise and shine" exhortation of Paul: "Wake up, O sleeper!" and live wisely, making the most of every opportunity, because the days are "evil" (Eph. 5:14-16).

Scriptural Examples

Samson. Samson slept both with his eyes and his mind as Delilah learned the secret of his miraculous strength, and cut off the seven braids of his hair. Those eyes that longed for sleep would soon be put out by the Philistines (Judg. 16:19-21).

Israel's watchmen. The Lord spoke of these leaders of Israel who were blind and lacked knowledge. They loved to sleep and lie around all day dreaming, never satisfied, as each sought his own way (Isa. 56:10-12).

Eutychus. This young man sat in a third story window listening to Paul preach. Sleep overcame him and he plunged to his death. Paul rushed down to him and restored him to life. Let's not be like Eutychus. Let's be watchful (Acts 20:9-12).

Prayer of Application

Father, teach me that I have only one life and it will soon pass; only what's done for Christ will last. Place my feet on the ground and give me the energy and strength to rise and shine every day.

Answer God's Call to Diligence

*Go to the ant, you sluggard; consider its ways and be wise! It has
no commander, no overseer or ruler, yet it stores its provisions in
summer and gathers its food at harvest. How long will you lie
there, you sluggard? When will you get up from your sleep? A little
sleep, a little slumber, a little folding of the hands to rest—and
poverty will come on you like a bandit and scarcity like
an armed man* (Prov. 6:6-11).

The ancient philosopher Seneca said, "It is a shame not to learn
morals from the small animals." Actually, it's a shame that people
made in the image of God need to observe tiny creatures for
instruction in righteousness. These little ants have no commander
to direct their work, no overseer to inspect their work, and no ruler
to call them into account. Yet they do their work diligently and in
proper order.

To make diligent use of the tools God has given us—our
minds, muscles, talents, educational opportunities, and, yes, our
knees—is to honor Him (Prov. 10:5; 24:27). Unlike the ants, we
have a commander and guide: the Holy Spirit. We have a ruler who
will one day call us into account. Yet, many of us still slack off in
the study of the Word, in the employment of our spiritual gifts,
and in our duties that fulfill the multiple roles in life to which God
has called us.

Avoid the way of the sluggard who is glued to her bed, or to her
favorite chair in front of the TV set. Let's use every day of our short
lives to honor God with our diligence.

Scriptural Examples

The temple builders. These diligent people rebuilt the temple
in Jerusalem. They made financial arrangements and hired work-
ers. They even finished the work under budget! The money left
over was used to make articles of service and for burnt offerings (2
Chron. 24:12-14). Let's be diligent like them!

Prayer of Application

Father, thank You for the lowly example of the ant and its
illustration of hard work and diligence. Help me to continually
practice good habits of that same work and diligence.

Honor God by Your Industry

Where there are no oxen, the manger is empty, but from the strength of the ox comes an abundant harvest (**Prov. 14:4**).

God formed Adam from the dust of the ground, and returned him to it to till it for food (Gen. 3:23). Mankind is required to work —be it on the job or at home—although it is God at work behind the scenes who provides for our needs. The psalmist speaks of God's providence, that He gives us food and satisfies our desires (Ps. 145:15-16). Jesus continues this theme in Matthew 6:26-33.

So in life, a partnership exists between God and us. Each has a role to play. Our responsibility is to labor in the field (or in the home), while God provides the field, sends the rain and the sunshine, and creates the botanical system. God has also created tools for our use, such as the ox in this proverb. Without oxen, one may have a clean stall, but there may be no dinner on the table.

This partnership is also at work in spiritual things. Although God saves a person by His sovereign power, we have the responsibility to follow Him in faith and to diligently study the Word and apply its truth to our lives. Whatever our role in life, let's honor God with our industry.

Scriptural Examples

Joseph. Joseph's administration of Egypt's storehouses filled them to overflowing. Then, when the famine came by God's providential hand, there was plenty for the people to eat. Joseph's industry and willingness to follow God figured prominently in the foundation of Israel (Gen. 41:49).

Elisha. Elijah found him industriously plowing his fields, using twelve yoke of oxen. He called him from the field to the service of God. Ultimately, Elisha became heir to the Spirit that rested upon the prophet of God (1 Kings 19:19-21).

Mary. One of several Marys whose work is noted in Scripture. This one was noted by Paul for her hard work (Rom. 16:6).

Prayer of Application

Father, thank You for Your great provision for every need that arises. Give me the strength, Lord, to be industrious in whatever You call me to do, to the end that You will be glorified in my life.

Set Realistic Goals and Work Toward Them

He who works his land will have abundant food, but the one who chases fantasies will have his fill of poverty (Prov. 28:19).

A good farmer will have his whole year planned. He knows exactly when to plow and sow and harvest and mend the fences and feed the animals. He has daily, weekly, monthly, and yearly goals that he sets for himself and his helpers. Then he gets up in the morning with one thought in mind: to accomplish what he has planned. He sets realistic goals and then goes to work. Each day he accomplishes just a little, so at harvest time his family's table is set for another year.

We've recently noticed that the things that have the most impact on our lives are those that require diligent, consistent effort —just one or two steps a day. You know—things like diet, exercise, changing old habits—and, of course, Bible study and prayer. Chasing fantasies is like always hoping something will "save us" from our circumstances—like winning the lottery—rather than realizing that our circumstances are from the Lord. He has provided different circumstances for each of us because He wants us to work with them and through them.

Set for yourself worthwhile goals in your business, family, physical, and spiritual lives, then work toward them diligently. God honors goals, and will take you places with them you never thought possible—one little step at a time.

Scriptural Examples

Solomon and the temple. Inheriting David's goal for the construction of a dwelling place for God, Solomon finished the drawings, planned the work, and built it. Solomon understood that it would be finished one step at a time (1 Kings 5:1–6:38).

Paul. Paul was a great goal-setter, and was undoubtedly the greatest church planter who has ever lived. How did he plant all of those churches? He did it one believer at a time.

Prayer of Application

Dear Lord, it seems so simple, but realistic goals are powerful. Thank You for setting the goal of the cross for Jesus, and for His work in marching toward that dark, yet joyous, hour.

Be Diligent in Your Work

One who is slack in his work is brother to one who destroys
(Prov. 18:9).

In St. Augustine's *Confessions*, he painfully recalls when he and some other boys stole some pears. The thing that troubled him deeply was that he wasn't hungry. It was pure vandalism. In San Diego, as elsewhere in our nation, vandalism is rampant. There are crushed mailboxes, graffiti, and broken windows. But what does this have to do with being diligent? The proverb says that the one who is slothful is a brother to the vandal.

In the world today, much more harm is done through sloth than vandalism. God has given each of us gifts and talents to employ. We need to honor God by diligently using them.

The same principle applies to our work in Christian service. We are called to diligence in worship (1 Chron. 22:19), the study of the Word (2 Tim. 2:15), obedience (Deut. 6:17), striving after perfection, (Phil. 3:13-14), good works (Eph. 2:10), and in making our calling more sure (1 Pet. 1:10)—indeed in all areas of life.

Scriptural Examples

The wise and foolish servants. Jesus tells of a master who left various sums of money in the care of his three servants. The first two put theirs to work immediately, and when the master returned, they both showed excellent profits. The third servant buried his in the ground. Then he accused his master of injustice, and excused himself on the grounds that he feared such injustice. He was cast into outer darkness (Matt. 25:14-30).

Dorcas. Also known as Tabitha, this godly woman was "always doing good and helping the poor." She was a maker of clothing. When she died unexpectedly, Peter raised her up (Acts 9:36-41).

Onesiphorus. Paul prayed to the Lord for mercy for this man's family. He had shown great diligence in searching for Paul in Rome, and in meeting his needs in jail (2 Tim. 1:16-17).

Prayer of Application

Lord, I pray that I might receive a real spirit of diligence in all of the tasks I am given to do. May I always remember to bring my brain to work, whatever the task, that I may use it as You intended.

Ponder the Results of Sloth

I went past the field of the sluggard, past the vineyard of the man who lacks judgment; thorns had come up everywhere, the ground was covered with weeds, and the stone wall was in ruins. I applied my heart to what I observed and learned a lesson from what I saw: A little sleep, a little slumber, a little folding of the hands to rest— and poverty will come on you like a bandit and scarcity like an armed man (Prov. 24:30-34).

One of the most beautiful settings in California is the Napa - Sonoma region, noted for its green, rolling hills and its fine wines. One may drive past mile after mile of beautiful vineyards, with brightly painted fences and precise stone walls. What a contrast to the vineyard in these verses! As Solomon says, "[I] learned a lesson from what I saw." Let's do the same.

Just like one's garden takes a persistent effort in its care and maintenance, so does every part of one's life. We might wonder also about this sluggard's home, his car, his job, his marriage, and his family. Would we see the same crumbling walls?

One relationship where sloth is often found is between ourselves and the Lord. Consistent Bible study, a vibrant prayer and devotional life, regular church attendance, participation in the Lord's supper, and fellowship with other believers are of inestimable worth if the Christian's "vineyard" is to bear fruit. If you neglect it, don't be surprised to see the thorns and thistles that grow up to choke out your fruitfulness. Ponder the results of sloth, and of slothful Christianity.

Scriptural Examples

The Lord's vineyard. Isaiah wrote of a day when the Lord's vineyard would bear much fruit, because the Lord Himself would watch over it. No briers or thorns will grow there. It will be a day when Jacob will take root, and all Israel will bud and blossom and fill all the world with its fruit (Isa. 27:2-6).

Prayer of Application

Father, how easy it is to slide back to old lazy ways. Help me to be more diligent in my relationship with You. That will bear godly fruit, and all of my other relationships will blossom, too.

Study Questions and Projects

1) Read Ecclesiastes 10:18. What does Solomon say are the results of laziness? Have you ever been lazy to such a degree that something like this happened to you? Share with others.

2) God has a few things to say about Israel's watchmen in Isaiah 56:10-12. To what animal does He compare them? What do they love to do? What does verse 11 say about their contentment? About their commitment to God? To what substance does it appear that they are addicted in verse 12? What do these verses teach us about people who are lazy and lack industriousness? Discuss with others.

3) Read Jesus' parable of the talents in Matthew 25:14-30. The master in the parable gave sums of money to three men. How many were wise and industrious in their use of what he had given them? Who was lazy and foolish? What excuse did he give for his inactivity? Of what does he accuse his master? How would you feel if you were on the receiving end of an accusation like that? To what does the master compare laziness in verse 26? What happens to the lazy servant?

4) What rule of life is given to us by the apostle Paul in 2 Thessalonians 3:10?

Other Verses to Study
Proverbs 10:4 and 21:5; Romans 12:11; 1 Thessalonians 4:11-12.

One to Memorize
He who works his land will have abundant food, but the one who chases fantasies will have his fill of poverty
(Prov. 28:19).

My Personal Action Plan to Be a Woman of Industry

1) _____ 2) _____

3) _____ 4) _____

- Proverbs 31:14 -
*She is like the merchant ships,
bringing her food from afar.*

Chapter Five

A Woman Who Plans
• •

Many people don't recognize the amount of work it takes to carry off a successful event. Think of a wedding, a dinner party, or a family vacation! It may seem as easy as pie, but only the planner knows the work that was involved.

The verse above compares the wise woman to "merchant ships, bringing her food from afar." Back in the days of Solomon, merchant ships were usually powered by a combination of sail and men who rowed. And they were very slow. Much planning had to go into any extended voyage. The crew had to eat and drink. Provision had to be made for the ship's welfare, such as extra sails and caulking to keep the water out. The course had to be planned, and the timing had to be precise to avoid winter storms. Even though transportation is much easier and quicker today, any mother with a toddler recognizes the planning needed for a trip.

All through the Bible, we see a God who has planned. He knew there would be a famine, so He sent Joseph down to Egypt to prepare. He knew we would need a Savior, so the Father planned and sent His Son to this earth to live and die for our sins. God, who knows the beginning from the end, is a planner. Can we do any less? We *must* plan, but leave all results in His gracious hands.

Make Plans to Do Good

Do not those who plot evil go astray? But those who plan what is good find love and faithfulness (Prov. 14:22).

To actually commit sin is wicked, but it is even greater wickedness to sin in premeditation. We know from our secular body of law that first-degree murder carries a much stiffer sentence than that of second degree, or murder without "malice aforethought." God hates the heart of the wicked schemer who goes astray in plotting evil (Prov. 6:16-18).

As children of God, our planning should be for the good. We will find the same principle at work. Just as the wicked person's plan heightened the sin, so the plan of the righteous woman for good heightens the righteousness of the deed. In fact, though the fruit of our work is often frustrated, God honors our righteous plans. God is interested more in the condition of our hearts than in our outward success.

And what is the reward for those who plan to do good? It is to "find love and faithfulness," or "truth and mercy" as the KJV translates the phrase. And what is this truth and mercy? It is none other than the blessedness of the Lord Jesus Christ. For as the law came through Moses, grace (mercy) and truth came through Jesus Christ (John 1:17).

Scriptural Examples

David. In contrast, this same David sent for Bathsheba in lust. When she became pregnant, David plotted to get her husband to sleep with his wife, so he would think the child was his. When this failed, David planned still even more evil. He had Uriah killed. David paid a great price for his evil plans (2 Sam. 11:3-17).

David. David wanted to build a temple in Jerusalem. God denied David that right, but told him his son Solomon would build it. David was honored by his plans, even though he never lived to see their fruition (1 Chron. 28:2-5; 1 Kings 8:18).

Prayer of Application

Dear Lord, guide me in the making of plans to further Your kingdom. I know that through You my godly plans will be successful, regardless of whether they bear fruit that I can see.

Let's Stop Making Excuses

A sluggard does not plow in season; so at harvest time he looks but finds nothing (**Prov. 20:4**).

It is estimated that in any given congregation, 10 percent of the membership does 90 percent of the work. It is also said that an even smaller percentage of members of evangelical churches in America tithe. No wonder we can't reach the lost for Christ, with the vast majority of Christians riding their hot-air balloons of excuses.

In this proverb we have a picture of the would-be farmer who can't plow his fields because it's too cold (see KJV). Frozen land is not the problem here. It's personal, not physical. He is uncomfortable plowing on those cold March mornings! He's procrastinating. Come harvest time, he'll look out at his fields and they'll still be brown dirt and weeds. No crops will have grown.

For many of us, procrastination is a habit that needs to be overcome. Not only are our plans and dreams stifled by it, but it brings depression and guilt in its wake. Let's stop making excuses and get on with the work at hand.

Scriptural Examples

Aaron. When Moses climbed the mountain, he left Aaron in charge of the camp. The people began to party, and Aaron made a golden calf. Aaron blamed his sin on the pressure of the people. He said the idol just popped out of the fire. Aaron is an example of our propensity to cook up an incredible excuse if the right excuse is wrong (Ex. 32:22-24).

Gideon. God chose Gideon to lead His people, but Gideon began coming up with excuses. He basically accused God of not being able to do what He said He would do (Judg. 6:12-17).

The unwilling disciples. These two men excused themselves from following Jesus. The first had to take care of his father, and the second wanted to bid his family good-bye. They placed personal priorities above the kingdom (Luke 9:59-62).

Prayer of Application

Father, forgive me for making excuses instead of being about Your work. Give me the wisdom to establish priorities, Lord, and then to make Your priorities my priorities.

Prepare for the Future in Diligence and Faith

*Be sure you know the condition of your flocks, give careful atten-
tion to your herds; for riches do not endure forever, and a crown is
not secure for all generations. When the hay is removed and new
growth appears and the grass from the hills is gathered in, the
lambs will provide you with clothing, and the goats with the price
of a field. You will have plenty of goats' milk to feed you and your
family and to nourish your servant girls* (**Prov.** 27:23-27).

We don't own any flocks or herds, not even a single goat. We
do have a modest portfolio of common stocks, but we've never
made it to the goal of "financial independence." Bob likes to say
that we could retire tomorrow, but only if we were to die next week.

The wealth of this world is fickle and fleeting (Matt. 6:19), and
in the final analysis, cannot be relied upon to provide us with so
much as a cup of coffee in the future. We are to rely upon God as
the ultimate source of all we have. He is absolutely reliable, and our
hearts can rest content in the knowledge that if all our investments
flop, our pension plan goes bankrupt, and the Social Security
system fails, God will provide for all our needs (Isa. 58:11; Phil.
4:19). But does this knowledge preclude us from being diligent
about providing for the future? These verses pronounce an em-
phatic "No!" We are to provide diligently for the future.

Scriptural Examples

Boaz. Boaz personally looked after his flocks and fields, not
leaving his future to chance. He exercised diligence in his work and
in his provision for the future (Ruth 2:1-16; 3:6-13).

The widow of Zarephath and Elijah. She said she only had
enough food for that day. After that, her meager supply would be
gone and she and her son would starve. But Elijah told her not to be
afraid. God would supply her needs. Her little jar of flour and jug
of oil never ran dry until the Lord brought rain (1 Kings 17:7-16).

Prayer of Application

Dear Heavenly Father, help me to trust You only as the Great
Provider of all things. But then help me to do my part in providing
for myself, for my immediate family, and for others in need.

Prepare for Change

The prudent see danger and take refuge, but the simple keep going and suffer for it (Prov. 27:12).

Many times we get so focused on the details of life that we fail to see the big picture. We need to lift our heads up and get a better understanding of where things are headed—in our own families, in our work, and in the nation and world.

It used to be—when things around us moved more slowly—that we could expect our jobs to last us our whole life. Today, we can't expect our husbands or ourselves to keep the same job until retirement. Technology keeps pushing forward, creating many new jobs, but eliminating many in its wake. We must be prepared for the future, and we must help our children to do the same. If the Lord does not come soon, they will see change that will make the current days seem like the "horse and buggy" days.

What can we do to prepare? The first thing that should be done is to seek the Lord's help. He alone will provide for all our needs. But we also must be wise. First, discover your hidden gifts, talents, and interests. How can they be used in the future? What training can you invest in now that will pay dividends later on? Seek counseling. Whatever you do, don't hide your head in the sand. Technological advances and change are here to stay.

Scriptural Examples

The inhabitants of Jerusalem. Jesus warned of a day when Jerusalem would be totally destroyed. The event occurred in A.D. 70 when Titus besieged the city and leveled it. The Christians who lived there and who heeded the warnings escaped. The simple minded who refused to see the danger ahead came into unbelievable suffering and death (Matt. 24:15-21).

Mary, mother of Jesus. Can you imagine the shock of being told, as a virgin, that you would give birth? Mary took it in stride and prepared for the future event (Luke 1:26-56).

Prayer of Application

Dear Lord, thank You that I do not have to worry about the future. But I am to make godly plans for my family's welfare. Help me to diligently prepare for the days ahead.

Go to Battle Armed with Good Advice

*Make plans by seeking advice; if you wage war,
obtain guidance* (Prov. 20:18).

In our lifetimes we have seen our U.S. presidents struggle often with decisions when war hung in the balance. Any such decision is an agonizing one and only made after the counsel of many advisers. Neither one of us would want to be faced with the responsibility of sending young men and women into armed conflict.

But every Christian is engaged in spiritual warfare (Phil. 1:29-30), so we see this proverb in that light. Each Christian needs to establish his or her own personal strategy in the struggle against Satan and his minions who would make war with God. We should do this armed with godly counsel. There are as many different roles in the battle as there are soldiers. Some will fight in foxholes along the front lines, while others will be engaged in supplying the front line troops with bread, prayer, and encouragement. Our roles are *all* vital. We all rely upon one another in the struggle.

Each one's calling in the battle plan will be in accordance with the gifts God has given him or her and should be established in the counsel of the Word of God. It should also be in the counsel of the wise advice of our pastors, elders, and other mature warriors of the faith. Take your place in the battle, and let the glory go to the One who has already won the victory!

Scriptural Examples

David. At war with the Philistines, David sought the counsel of God as to whether or not to attack. God said that he should, so David attacked and was victorious. But then the enemy entered the Valley of Rephaim. David once more inquired of God. This time, the Lord gave him tactical instructions. David was to circle around behind enemy lines, and as soon as he heard the sound of marching, he was to attack. David won again (2 Sam. 5:17-25).

Prayer of Application

Father, You have drafted me into Your army for spiritual warfare. Help me to take up Your battle cry and, armed with advice from Your Word and godly Christians, go daily into the fray.

Rest in the Providence of God

Commit to the Lord whatever you do, and your plans will succeed
(**Prov. 16:3**).

Paul enjoins us in Philippians 4:6-7 not to be anxious about anything, but to pray with thanksgiving, that our hearts may be guarded with the peace of God that passes all natural understanding. The key to this peace is absolute trust and confidence in God. Proverbs 3:5-6 reiterates this principle of trust in God.

First, we must understand the God in whom we are called to trust. He is absolutely sovereign and is able to do much more than we give Him credit for. He is subordinate to none. Second, the faith we have in God must be an active faith. It is praying with thanksgiving and believing God hears us, that whatever we ask of Him, He can do (Mark 11:24). Finally, it is a faith that steps out with humble trust in the love, power, and provision of God. It is a faith that prays and then goes to work.

The woman who commits the works of her hands, mind, and heart to the glory and honor of the Lord Jesus knows that her steps, plans, and even her every thought will be established and rewarded with eternal treasure in heaven (1 Cor. 3:11-15).

Scriptural Examples

Eliezer. Abraham's servant searched for a bride for Isaac. He committed his way to the Lord and his plans succeeded. He found and brought back Rebekah for his master's son (Gen. 24).

Nehemiah. He prayed that God would help in obtaining approval to rebuild Jerusalem. God established Nehemiah's way and work, and the city was restored (Neh. 1:4-11).

Daniel. Daniel purposed in his heart not to defile himself with the king's food but to follow the law of the Lord. God caused the officials in the king's palace to show favor to Daniel and his friends, Shadrach, Meshach, and Abednego. Because of their faith in the God of Israel, their ways were established (Dan. 1:8-9).

Prayer of Application

Provident Lord, help me to trust You fully in all things. I often want to trust in my own resources, and that is idolatry. Cause me to pray fervently, and then to work just as fervently.

Study Questions and Projects

1) In 2 Corinthians 8 and 9, Paul interrupts his message to Corinth regarding the defense of his apostleship to insert a practical example of his leadership in the Christian community. He has been planning a collection for the church in Jerusalem.

a) Whom does Paul say began the planning for the collection among the Corinthian church?

b) What does Paul urge the Corinthians to do in 8:11? How are "willingness" and "completion" related? Discuss with others.

c) Who put into the heart of Titus the desire to plan what was going on and then to work his plan? (8:16)

d) What act is Paul planning in 8:19? What had the Corinthians been planning for a year or more in 9:2? What is Paul exhorting them to do in 9:3?

e) What does Paul's statement in 9:7 have to do with your planning today? Your church's planning?

f) In 9:10-11, Paul refers to the real source of the Corinthians' ability to plan and to give. Who is it?

g) What other benefits does Paul promise will flow from the Corinthians' planning and "giving" or "working" in 9:12-15?

Other Verses to Study

Job 42:2; Proverbs 21:30; Amos 3:7; Ephesians 1:11.

One to Memorize

Commit to the Lord whatever you do, and your plans will succeed (Prov.16:3).

My Personal Action Plan to Be a Woman Who Plans

1) _____ 2) _____

3) _____ 4) _____

Chapter Six

A Woman Who Prays
•••••••••••••••••••••••••••••

Have you ever heard the saying, "The ground is level at the foot of the cross"? It was originally intended to mean, "Whosoever wants to come to Jesus is welcome." That is very true. But we believe its application is much wider. It also means, "Every Christian is on equal ground at the cross of Christ when he or she comes to God in believing prayer." The call to prayer is the most important calling in the world, and it matters not about your gifts, intelligence, social position, good looks, degrees, office, financial net worth, color, marital status, denomination, or any other earthly distinction we people make between one another.

Prayer is our highest calling, and our greatest privilege. No other religion in the world can offer what biblical Christianity offers. Our gracious God commands that we speak to Him personally. We can only assume that the woman in these verses arose, "while it [was] still dark," to seek His face. She's that kind of woman! In prayer we give God our adoration, we tell Him our troubles and concerns, we thank Him for supplying all our needs, and we confess our sins to receive His forgiveness. In short, He becomes for us a friend like no other. He loves us unconditionally and calls us to rest in Him. Imagine! The God who created the universe wants to talk with us! Wow! Why don't we pray more?

Seek God in Your Daily Quiet Time

Now then, my sons, listen to me; blessed are those who keep my ways. Listen to my instruction and be wise; do not ignore it. Blessed is the man who listens to me, watching daily at my doors, waiting at my doorway. For whoever finds me finds life and receives favor from the Lord. But whoever fails to find me harms himself; all who hate me love death (**Prov. 8:32-36**).

Jesus said in Luke 9:23, "If anyone would come after me, he must deny himself and take up his cross daily and follow me." In Galatians 2:20, Paul says that we have been crucified with Christ, and we no longer live unto ourselves. Christ has become the central focus and purpose of the Christian's new life, a life that is lived by faith in Him. We can bear our cross only by faith, and we are to live moment by moment in it, from faith to faith, step by step, on a daily basis (Rom. 1:17).

These verses state two of the great blessings that have been promised to the person who will listen to the instruction of God's wisdom and keep God's ways. He will find life and favor (grace) from the Lord. These come by watching daily at His feet and waiting at His doorway (Rev. 3:20).

Those who say "I'm too busy" or "I don't have the time" to meet with God are really saying, "My priorities don't allow time for You today, Lord." If your boss asked for a 30-minute meeting each morning, could you find the time? Just as we need food daily to meet our physical needs (Matt. 6:11), so also do we need our daily feeding from the Vine of spiritual food. Without it you'll be a frail and fruitless Christian. Beginning today, let's get our priorities straight. Let's seek God first—in His Word and in prayer.

Scriptural Examples

The Bereans. The Bereans examined the Scriptures to see if what Paul said was true. What's more, the Scripture tells us that they did it on a daily basis (Acts 17:11).

Prayer of Application

Dear Lord, provider of all rich things for our enjoyment, help me to recognize You as the giver of all things, and to make time for prayer and for Your Word on a daily basis.

Pray to Your Father Who Hears You

The Lord is far from the wicked but he hears the prayer of the righteous (Prov. 15:29).

God's presence fills the universe, so in that sense He is equally near every person on the planet (Acts 17:27-28). But in His gracious favor, He hears and answers the prayers of believers. At the crucifixion of Jesus, the curtain of the temple was torn in two (Matt. 27:51), and the way into God's presence was opened for us. What a great privilege we have in prayer!

Our duty as Christians is to pray always (1 Thess. 5:17). Our heavenly Father will not bar access to His seeking child. Rather, He is only too willing to give us the things we ask of Him, in His timing, and in accordance with His will. But let your prayers have a definite object in mind. Then make sure your motives are right, and that you are not praying selfishly to bring yourself pleasure, without profit for others or glory for God. Finally, have full confidence in the One who hears and responds. The prayer of faith is powerful and effective (James 5:17).

Scriptural Examples

The Israelites. The Lord turned a deaf ear to the people of Israel following their decision at Kadesh Barnea to fight the Amorites in their own strength. God wouldn't bless their works done in the flesh (Deut. 1:45).

The enemies of David. As David praised the Lord for deliverance, he recounted how his enemies and Saul had prayed to the Lord but were not heard (Ps. 18:40-41).

David. David testified that the Lord had heard his prayer and had delivered him from trouble (Ps. 116:1-7).

The saints who prayed for Paul. Paul was delivered from sickness and death, and gave testimony to the effectiveness of the prayers of the saints who stood with him, and to the graciousness of the Lord in answering them (2 Cor. 1:9-11).

Prayer of Application

Father, teach me what it means to pray in faith, persistently believing that You will answer my prayer. Create in me a prayerful spirit, that I will thankfully bring all things to You.

Cry Out to God for His Wisdom

My son, if you accept my words and store up my commands within you, turning your ear to wisdom and applying your heart to understanding, and if you call out for insight and cry aloud for understanding, and if you look for it as silver and search for it as for hidden treasure, then you will understand the fear of the Lord and find the knowledge of God (**Prov. 2:1-5**).

These verses are a treasure map for the greatest treasure imaginable. The directional arrows are the verbs found in these verses. Notice them. First, the treasure hunter needs to *accept* wisdom's words (1a). The serious student will diligently study God's Word and receive it by faith as truth. Next, she is to *store up* commandments within her (1b). She is to hide the Word in her heart (Ps. 119:11). Then, the student of the Word *turns her ear* to wisdom (2a), and *applies her heart* to understanding (2b). This is not academic research, but a spiritual quest. Then in verse 3, we find the student on her knees *crying out* in prayer for understanding and insight (James 1:5). Finally (4), she keeps on *looking* and *searching* for it as hidden treasure (Matt. 7:7).

And what is the treasure that the student so diligently seeks? It is to know the One True God. And how shall we know Him? We will find that His name is Jesus, who is one with "El Shaddai" and "Yahweh" of fearsome majesty. He is our shield, and our exceeding great reward (Gen. 15:1). He is the treasure, hidden from the world (2 Cor. 4:3-4), but revealed to those who would seek Him in His Word and in prayer. He is, in fact, wisdom personified (Prov. 8; 1 Cor. 1:30).

Scriptural Examples

Anna. This 84-year-old widow was living in the temple when Jesus visited it as a boy. We're told that she never left the place, but continually fasted and prayed. Anna recognized Jesus for who He was, "the redemption of Jerusalem" (Luke 2:36-38).

Prayer of Application

Father, how I want to know Jesus, to fix my thoughts upon Him and find the treasure of joy that He has for me. Dear God, supply me with the wisdom that can only be found in Christ.

Beware of Mocking God

If anyone turns a deaf ear to the law, even his
prayers are detestable (Prov. 28:9).

Prayer is an unspeakable privilege. As these words flow from our minds and fingers to the computer screen, we are shivering inside. Oh, that we were more a man and woman of prayer. We must confess that we are not nearly what we should be. But we know that when we pray, God is faithful to hear and answer our prayer because we love His law and try to apply it to our lives. Do we always do so? Sadly we do not, but we *want* to (Rom. 7:15-21).

This proverb addresses the person who will not even *listen* to the law of God. That is, she will not open God's Word and read it, and then prayerfully seek to make it the grid through which all her thoughts, words, and actions are judged. In short, she couldn't care less about what God has to say, although ironically she thinks God should care about what she has to say. She wants the benefits of knowing God with none of the responsibility. The prayers of such a person are detestable to God.

Are you like the person who turns a deaf ear to God? If so, you might like to know of the exception to the rule of the proverb above. God will hear the prayer of the repentant heart. Confess your idolatry to God and He will hear from heaven and forgive you (1 Kings 8:33-39; 2 Chron. 7:14).

Scriptural Examples

The elders of Israel. These men came to Ezekiel to seek the Lord. The Lord would not allow them to inquire of Him because the idolatry of their fathers was continuing (Ezek. 20).

Simon the sorcerer. This man was practicing witchcraft in Samaria when he heard the gospel through Phillip. When Peter and John came up from Jerusalem, Simon, wishing to use the Holy Spirit as a tool to increase his sorcery business, offered to pay the apostles for the gift of the Spirit. Peter rebuked him (Acts 8:9-24).

Prayer of Application

Dear God, thank You for the privilege of prayer. Help me, Lord, to be a woman of much prayer. But I understand that if I won't listen to You and Your law, neither will You listen to me.

Beware of Shutting Your Ears to the Poor

If a man shuts his ears to the cry of the poor, he too will cry out and not be answered (**Prov. 21:13**).

In our city, as in other communities across the nation, the problem of feeding the poor and homeless has become widespread. But our government's welfare system often locks the poor into a system of handouts and provides little incentive or ability to find meaningful employment. Such welfare is a sinful system that concerned Christians should challenge.

Our church is active in a rescue mission that gives food, clothing, and a gospel message to all who come. Other Christian works we support help the needy in our society. They should be supported with our money and our time. Beware of the proverb's warning. To shut one's ears to the cry of the poor will bring God's judgment. We will cry out to Him, but we will not be heard.

Just as Proverbs 28:9 warns about God's ears being deaf to those who spurn His law, so too does He shut His ears to those who shut out the cries of the poor and needy. When we do that, we are guilty of the words of Isaiah quoted by Jesus in Matthew 15:8: "These people honor me with their lips, but their hearts are far from me." Let us worship Him in spirit and in truth.

Scriptural Examples

Job and Eliphaz. Job's friend Eliphaz accused him of shutting his ears to the poor (Job 22:7), and ascribed part of the reason for the calamity that had come upon Job to that sin. Job was confident that he was innocent of the charges. He was (Job 31:7).

The rich man and Lazarus. For years, the beggar Lazarus had lain at the gate of the rich man, who wouldn't give the poor homeless man the time of day. Both died. The rich man cried out from hell for Lazarus to put only a drop of water on his tongue. His cries for mercy went unanswered (Luke 16:19-31).

Prayer of Application

Lord, make me more sensitive to the needs of the poor in our society. Help me to serve them, to the end that Your kingdom may come, Your will may be done, and my prayer may be heard.

Pray for God's Control Over Your Life

Two things I ask of you, O Lord; do not refuse me before I die:
Keep falsehood and lies far from me; give me neither poverty nor
riches, but give me only my daily bread. Otherwise, I may have too
much and disown you and say, "Who is the Lord?" Or I may
become poor and steal, and so dishonor the name of my God
(Prov. 30:7-9).

A man named Agur penned these verses. Because he says in verse 7, "before I die," it seems to me that this was Agur's "life prayer." Do you have a "life prayer" like you may have a "life verse"? If not, you might want to adopt Agur's. He asks for only two things. First, he asks to be kept from falsehood and lies. The world system is a system of lies, of self-seeking deception. It says it will do what only God can do and leads many astray. How different is God's way, the way of humility and truth. Agur is a man of humility and we see it clearly in his prayer.

The second part of Agur's prayer is strange indeed. How many people do you know who pray that they may be kept from riches? Most of us see riches as a blessing of God. But Agur knew that often the more material wealth a person has, the less she thinks she needs God. Then in verse 8 he asks that he also be kept from poverty. He feared he would become a thief under those circumstances.

Agur wants simply to bring honor to the name of his God (9b). This should be the motivating force behind every Christian's life (1 Cor. 10:31; Phil. 2:11). Each of us should pray that God will control every detail of our lives, then submit fully to His providential care. That is the need of every Christian.

Scriptural Examples

Jeshurun. The name "Jeshurun" is a pseudonym for Israel. In Deuteronomy 32:15 we find that Jeshurun grew fat and sleek and was filled with food. He abandoned God his Savior, which is exactly what Agur had feared in his prayer.

Prayer of Application

Father, I want to adopt Agur's prayer as my own. I have seen what riches and poverty can do to people, and I'm afraid of both. Control every part of my life, Lord, that I might walk in Your ways.

Study Questions and Projects

1) In our study, we ran across two proverbs—21:13 and 28:9—that gave us reasons why God sometimes does not answer prayer. What other reasons do the following verses give us for God's shutting His ears to our prayer?

    a) Psalm 66:18

    b) Proverbs 1:24-28

    c) Isaiah 1:15

    d) Micah 3:4

    e) Zechariah 7:12-13

    f) John 9:31

    g) James 1:6; 4:3

    h) 1 Peter 3:7

2) Perhaps the greatest prayer in the Bible is found in John 17. For what is Jesus praying? Do you think His prayer was answered? Has it been effective in your life? Discuss with others.

3) What do the prayers of 1 Kings 17:21 and John 11:41-42 have in common?

4) What secrets of prayer does Jesus give us in:

    a) Matthew 6:5-15?

    b) Matthew 7:7-12?

    c) Luke 18:1-8?

Other Verses to Study

Psalms 5:1-3; Ecclesiastes 5:2; Philippians 4:6.

One to Memorize

If anyone turns a deaf ear to the law, even his prayers are detestable
(Prov. 28:9).

My Personal Action Plan to Be a
Woman Who Prays

1) _____ 2) _____

3) _____ 4) _____

- Proverbs 31:15b -
She provides food for her family
and portions for her servant girls.

Chapter Seven

A Woman of Justice

• •

The wise woman of Proverbs 31 treats all people the same. Here, we see that just as she provides for her own family, she respects the needs of her employees, too. Jesus' Golden Rule of Matthew 7:12 "sums up the Law and the Prophets." He said, "So in everything, do to others what you would have them do to you." That is exactly what she is doing.

The law of God relating to fairness and justice is really quite simple when you look at it in terms of the Golden Rule—its lowest common denominator. Just think of the way you would want to be treated in a certain situation, and then go ahead and treat your neighbor like *that*. If you would expect to be paid fairly in a certain job, then if you are the boss, make sure your employees are paid fairly. If you expect a 100 percent effort from others, be sure to give 100 percent yourself. If you take offense at being gossiped about, never gossip about others.

In this chapter we'll look at some proverbs dealing with treating others fairly. It is of special interest to God as you might suspect. He said in Jeremiah 9:24, "I am the Lord, who exercises kindness, justice and righteousness on earth, for in these I delight."

Exercise Authority in Justice and Truth

These also are the sayings of the wise: To show partiality in judging is not good: Whoever says to the guilty, "You are inno-cent"—peoples will curse him and nations denounce him. But it will go well with those who convict the guilty, and rich blessing will come upon them. An honest answer is like a kiss on the lips (**Prov. 24:23-26**).

Someone says, "Wait a second, I'm not a judge! I don't have any authority over people! How does this principle apply to me?" We're glad you asked. Are you a parent? Elected to an office at school or church? Supervise others at work? A hospital volunteer? Virtually every person in the world exercises some kind of authority over others at one time or another. These proverbs are aimed at that rather large group of people.

From almost the moment we are able to speak, we humans know the words "that's not fair!" We all have an innate sense of fair play, and when it is offended we get very upset. We believe God is calling us in these proverbs to a strict duty of fair play—without partiality—where the wronged party gets justice.

God wants us to be a people of justice and truth. Whatever your position or calling, honest and forthright dealings with those under your authority are always the best policy. In fact, an honest and upright policy is just like a kiss on the lips.

Scriptural Examples

Joel and Abijah. These sons of Samuel accepted bribes and perverted justice. The people of Israel were very angry and cried out against their unrighteous rule (1 Sam. 8:1-3).

David's oracle. His last words bring tribute to those who reign in righteousness and in the fear of God (2 Sam. 23:1-4).

Job. Job sat by the city gate in the place of judgment and was revered by the people. He said "I put on righteousness as my clothing and justice was my robe and my turban" (Job 29:7-17).

Prayer of Application

Father, how often it seems that fair play turns unfair under the influence of sin. Help me to be fair in every way, particularly when You have put me in a position of authority over others.

Treat the Poor with Justice and Equity

The poor man and the oppressor have this in common: The Lord
gives sight to the eyes of both. If a king judges the poor with fairness,
his throne will always be secure (Prov. 29:13-14).

At first glance, these proverbs seem to deal with two different issues. The first says that God has made all people equal in His sight (Prov. 22:2), while the second instructs kings how to maintain their thrones. But the verses' real commonality is that they both deal with ways of treating the poor. In verse 13, the poor are oppressed. In verse 14, they are treated fairly.

One thing characterizes the poor of every generation: their disenfranchisement. They have very little power in making social change. If oppressed, they rarely have an alternative but to bear it. What their foolish oppressor fails to realize is that the poor are his equals in God's sight. God gives sight, and life, to all. The only real difference is the disparity of wealth and position, both of which are within the providential oversight of God. So, what we have is a person who foolishly uses God-given power to oppress those who have no power. This is utmost foolishness in the sight of God.

Conversely, the wise king (or citizen) sees the poor as family and as a responsibility before God. He therefore treats them as God would lead him to treat them—with justice and equity. He is blessed by God and reigns securely.

Scriptural Examples

King Solomon. He asked the Lord for a discerning mind so that he would be able to apply just principles in his reign. His reign is a type of the reign of a King who will come again to bring judgment upon all oppressors (2 Chron. 1:9-13).

King Jesus. It is King Jesus who sits upon that throne. What Solomon could not do because of his weakness, Jesus will do forever in perfect righteousness and justice. Foolish oppressors beware. Even now He reigns! (Ps. 9; Heb. 1: 8-9; Rev. 22).

Prayer of Application

Lord, thank You that Jesus reigns, and will reign eternally. We see much injustice toward the poor. Help me to move counter to this world's ways and be a representative of the King.

Seek Justice in a World of Injustice

*It is not good to be partial to the wicked or to deprive
the innocent of justice* (Prov. 18:5).

God showed how deeply He is concerned with justice when
He sent Jesus to the cross to pay the just penalty for our sins. He
did not set aside justice in granting us mercy. That should strike
terror in the heart of non-believers. Without Christ, justice means
eternal punishment for them.

The following examples all surround events in and near a city
of Manasseh, which had a history related to the theme of justice.

Scriptural Examples

Dinah and the Shechemites. The sons of Jacob dealt cruelly
and unjustly with the people of Shechem following their sister's
seduction by Shechem, son of Hamor (Gen. 34:1-30).

Joseph and Dotham. Jacob sent Joseph to the vicinity of
Dotham to look for his brothers. On his arrival, they threw him
into a dry cistern, then sold him into slavery (Gen. 37:12-28).

Shechem—city of refuge. As a "city of refuge," Shechem
would serve justice as a protection of those accused of murder until
their innocence or guilt could be proven (Josh. 20:7).

Joshua and Shechem. Joshua called the people there to decide
if they would serve the Lord of justice or foreign gods. The people
chose the Lord, so Joshua put up a monument against them should
they prove to be untrue (Josh. 24:1-28).

Abimelech and Shechem. Gideon's son unjustly murdered his
seventy brothers at Ophrah. He was crowned king by the people
of Shechem before being mortally wounded (Judg. 9).

Rehoboam and Shechem. Solomon's son made himself king
in Shechem and promised to deal unjustly with the people. The
kingdom was ultimately divided (1 Kings 12:1-24; 14:21-31).

Murderers near Shechem. Hosea told of marauders who
murdered people on the road to Shechem (Hos. 6:9).

Prayer of Application

Father, thank You for sending Christ to die on the cross to pay
the penalty for my sins. Help me to emulate Your passion for
justice, Lord, by living my life in obedience to Your Word.

Know the Joy of Peace with God

An evil man is snared by his own sin, but a righteous one can sing and be glad. The righteous care about justice for the poor, but the wicked have no such concern (Prov. 29:6-7).

Verse seven is merely an illustration of the truth of verse six. We've all seen evil people merrily singing away, but their gladness is shallowly anchored in mud. They live only for themselves. They go their merry way, unaware of the trap being set. On the other hand, the righteous woman is anchored on the Rock, the sure hope of salvation in Jesus Christ (Heb. 6:18-20). Her song of gladness stems from her being at peace with God. Because of this peace, she cares about justice. Her gladness and joy will be eternal.

How does peace with God manifest itself now? First, there is a sense of *harmony* between the Christian and God. Fear has lost its grip. She is calm and stable, no longer at war with God or her neighbor. Second, the Christian has a sense of *adequacy*, of knowing that Christ has promised to fill all of her needs and never to leave or forsake her. Third, there is a sense of *freedom*, as she is no longer enslaved by sin. She has a clear conscience and knows that God has forgiven her and has the power to keep her from falling. Finally, there is an overarching sense of *purpose* to her life. She knows that every moment has eternal consequences, and so she is not lost in meaninglessness. She therefore seeks justice for the poor and for all people.

Scriptural Examples

The blessed of the Father. Jesus told of a day when His sheep would be separated from the goats. Then the blessed of the Father will be given their long-awaited inheritance. Christ said that His sheep are those who fed and clothed Him, who visited Him in sickness and in prison. "When did we do this, Lord?" they will ask. Christ will respond in that day, "Whatever you did for the least of these brothers of mine, you did for me" (Matt. 25:34-40).

Prayer of Application

Lord, before I knew You, I reveled in shallow self-interest. But You opened my eyes to the trap. Thank You for the peace that floods my heart and grows more each day as I learn of You.

Weigh All of the Facts

He who answers before listening—that is his folly and his shame
(**Prov. 18:13**).

When we used to read this proverb, we thought it dealt with finishing other people's sentences. But there is a much deeper meaning here regarding proper judgments. The fool believes anything she's told (Prov. 14:15; 17:4), and because of her pride her mind is unlikely to be changed when faced with the facts.

Like any business organization, our company has had its share of rumor mongers in the past who stirred up dissension. During a siege of such gossip a few years ago, we established "Operation Truth," a program roughly derived from Matthew 18:15-18. When gossip is heard, the hearer is to take the talebearer to his or her immediate superior, where the tale is to be traced back to its beginning, and the truth discovered. It worked well.

Listen carefully to all parties involved. Probe for salient facts as opposed to mere opinions. Apart from that depth of investigation, don't believe anything you hear from a gossip.

Scriptural Examples

Solomon. He listened carefully to each side disputing the motherhood of a baby. He asked a probing question, the answer to which made all the difference (1 Kings 3:16-28).

Zophar the Naamathite. Job's friends unjustly accused him regarding the source of his troubles. It was partly due to their failure to listen and weigh all of the facts (Job 20:1-3; 21:1-6).

The crowd in Jerusalem. Paul spoke to this hostile crowd. They listened quietly until he said that God had sent him to take the gospel to the Gentiles, then they went berserk (Acts 22:1-24).

The Great Judge. God is patient and forebearing, but He is saving up our every word and deed (Matt. 12:36) for the day when He will open up the books and call everyone to the eternal court of law (Heb. 4:13; Rom. 14:10b).

Prayer of Application

Dear Lord, so often my sinful mind wants to judge something before I have weighed all of the facts. Keep me from prejudging, Lord, and instead to distrust any gossip I may hear.

Have Faith in God and His Justice

Do not say, "I'll pay you back for this wrong!" Wait for the Lord,
and he will deliver you (Prov. 20:22).

One of the most cherished of all human lusts is the lust for revenge. When we sense we have been wronged, such as being cut off on the freeway, our first instinct may be to lash out in an attempt to see justice done. When we do so, we sin, and the justice of God is not done. Throughout Scripture we see examples of this. Simeon and Levi sought vengeance for the seduction of their sister Dinah (Gen. 34). Moses murdered the soldier in Egypt (Ex. 2:11-14). Joab vengefully slaughtered Abner (2 Sam. 3:27).

Personal revenge is expressly forbidden by God (Lev. 19:18; Rom. 12:17). Why? Because God says that He alone is the instrument of revenge (Rom. 12:19). He has established government to be his "agent of wrath" in administering justice (Rom. 13:4). Only God knows a person's motives, and since we are prejudiced toward our own position, we will have a tendency to inflict worse punishment than justice calls for.

Paul says that instead of repaying evil for evil, we are to repay evil with good (Rom. 12:20-21). In this way we will reflect the love of Christ and fulfill our position and calling as God's ministers of reconciliation (2 Cor. 5:18-21).

Scriptural Examples

Shimei and David. This relative of Saul sat by the side of the road and cursed David, pelting him with stones. Abashai suggested that Shimei's head be removed, but David said the Lord would see and bring justice (2 Sam. 16:5-14).

Herodias. Herodias married her brother-in-law, Herod, and received the scorn of John the Baptist. She held a grudge against John and looked for revenge. At a feast, her daughter danced for Herod and his guests, and was given one request. At her mother's prompting, John was decapitated (Mark 6:19-24).

Prayer of Application

Lord God, often on the freeway I feel endangered by someone's erratic driving and want to exact revenge. Help me to be calm, to back off and to let You and the police handle it.

Study Questions and Projects

1) Read Exodus 18:21. What two requirements for judges, or rulers, does God set forth here? Why are these qualities important in the administration of justice on earth?

2) Leviticus 19:15 gives us more principles that apply to judging fairly. What are they? Can you think of instances in our society when these precepts have been broken?

3) In Deuteronomy 19:16-19, what was the penalty for a person who witnessed falsely against his neighbor ? Do you think that would be a good law for America? Which of the Ten Commandments given in Exodus 20 would such a false witness break?

4) According to Proverbs 29:26, where is our final court of appeal for justice and equity?

5) According to Jesus' words in Matthew 5:23-24, how important is it that we treat others justly? Have you treated someone else unfairly? Did giving your tithe or offering remind you of it? What did you do?

Other Verses to Study

Psalms 72:1-2; Proverbs 17:15 and 18:17; Ecclesiastes 3:16-17;
1 Corinthians 13:6.

One to Memorize

An evil man is snared by his own sin, but a righteous one can sing and be glad. The righteous care about justice for the poor, but the wicked have no such concern (Prov. 29:6-7).

My Personal Action Plan to Be a Woman of Justice

1) _____ 2) _____

3) _____ 4) _____

- Proverbs 31:16 -
She considers a field and buys it;
out of her earnings she plants a vineyard.

Chapter Eight

A Woman of Financial Wisdom

As you have no doubt noticed by now, this woman of Proverbs 31 is someone really special. Could any one person possibly measure up to her? We doubt it. But she is someone whom we all, both men and women, can try to emulate.

Here we see her in her role as a capitalist —a real entrepreneur. She knows the secret to wealth. She has purchased a field and out of her earnings plants a vineyard. Next year she will be shopping for an apple orchard! Not all of us are called to be financial "movers and shakers." However, that does not preclude us from using our talents and common sense to create wealth.

The real secret to wealth lies not in how much we earn, but in how much we *keep* of what we earn. We believe it all starts with the tithe. First, give 10 percent of what you earn to the Lord, who is the source of all we have, and who really owns all wealth in the final analysis. Then, *save* the second 10 percent. Small nest eggs turn into large nest eggs through the principal of compound interest. But that takes time. So start early, stay out of the consumer debt trap, invest wisely for the long haul, and be generous to God and to His people. Before you know it, you may want to buy a field and plant a vineyard!

Get Out of Debt

The rich rule over the poor, and the borrower is servant to the lender (Prov. 22:7).

Have you seen the bumper sticker that reads, "I owe, I owe, so off to work I go"? The American way seems to be to load up ourselves with a mountain of debt as we seek the "good life" here and now, not understanding its ultimate toll on us as we become enslaved to the payments.

Christian economist and financial advisor Larry Burkett includes this principle as a common thread throughout his advice to clients: Get out of debt, particularly consumer debt or debt that has been encountered in the purchase of rapidly depreciating assets. He views those assets differently from a house, which should have a measure of price stability.

The Christian who has indebtedness beyond a modest or necessary house payment is seeing his or her money go to interest each month that could otherwise be put to work in the Lord's service. Our credit card debt then becomes a two-edged sword. It cuts us in the direction of our servitude to the lender, and then in our lack of servanthood to the Lord (Matt. 6:24). The best way is to be debt-free, if you can pull it off. That should at least be a very practical goal for every Christian woman.

Scriptural Examples

The Egyptians. God honors the payment of debt. While in bondage to this nation for 400 years, the Israelites were owed plenty. On leaving they got repaid, as their prior captors reached down deep in their pockets (Ex. 12:36).

Slavery and the debtor's prison. In former times, and certainly in Old Testament times, actual slavery might be imposed on a debtor, should he default. In some civilizations debtors' prisons were common. Jesus alluded to this type of prison in Matthew 5:25-26. Debt creates a different form of slavery today.

Prayer of Application

Heavenly Father, help me to live within my means, giving back to You my tithes and offerings and being cautious in taking on any debt which could enslave me.

Put First Things First

Finish your outdoor work and get your fields ready; after that, build your house (**Prov.** 24:27).

This proverb makes us think of the pioneer family who comes upon a fine-looking plot of land and decides to settle down. They sleep in their covered wagon until they get the corn crop planted down by the river. Then they begin to build their home on high ground above the flood plain. But most of us aren't farmers, much less pioneers. How do these verses apply to us?

Several commentators see "house" here as referring to a family. They say that the verse is telling us to get financially and emotionally stable before getting married. That's exactly what the pioneer family was doing, although in another context. They planted the field so they would have something to put on the table when they built a house for the table. They put first things first. They had their priorities straight.

Actually, the verse above could have read, "First, get your medical degree, then do brain surgery." Or, "First, go to the gym, then buy that bathing suit." How about, "First, save the cash, then purchase the stereo." The principle is the same in all of these cases. Be sure you have what it takes to advance to the next step in your life, then go ahead.

Scriptural Examples

The tower builder. Our Lord told of the person who wanted to build a tower. He said that the smart thing to do is to sit down and figure out how much it is going to cost. If there is enough cash, go ahead and start building (Luke 14:28-30).

The church builder. In building the Lord's church the principle is the same: First, know that your foundation is solid, then build on it. Paul tells us that this foundation is none other than Jesus Christ and the gospel of salvation through faith alone (1 Cor. 3:10-15; Eph. 2:8-9).

Prayer of Application

Father God, help me to get my priorities straight. Remind me daily that my first priority is to seek Your glory and righteousness. Then all else that I need will be added unto me.

Be Careful of Equating Wealth with Blessing

*Better a poor man whose walk is blameless than a rich man whose
ways are perverse* (Prov. 28:6).

We recently read of a survey taken in our city where some of
the wealthy in an affluent bedroom community were interviewed
regarding the source of their riches. An overwhelming majority of
those interviewed said that they definitely believed they were rich
because God had blessed the character and content of their lives
with material prosperity. Now they were right in assuming that
their wealth came from God's providence, but they were not
necessarily right in assuming that their wealth was a blessing of
God. It could very well be a curse.

Jesus said, "It is easier for a camel to go through the eye of a
needle than for a rich man to enter the kingdom of God" (Matt.
19:23-24). His disciples were astounded. They carried with them
the belief that God must have enriched the rich man because of his
piety or excellent character. But riches can make us disown God
(Prov. 30:9). For as James tells us, "Has not God chosen those who
are poor in the eyes of the world to be rich in faith and to inherit
the kingdom he promised those who love him?" (James 2:5). The
rich woman whose ways are perverse, and who is looking for her
treasure on this earth and not in heaven, is infinitely poorer than
the poor woman who has Christ.

Scriptural Examples

The rich man and Lazarus. By all appearances, the high living
rich man was blessed of God in his wealth, while the homeless
beggar was the scourge of the earth. But in the final analysis, their
roles switched, and for eternity (Luke 16:19-31).

The poor widow. While rich men were putting their 10
percent into the temple treasury, this woman gave 100 percent —
all she had. Her trust was rightly grounded in the Living God, and
not in her meager coins (Luke 21:1-4; Matt. 6:3).

Prayer of Application

Father, thank You for providing my material needs. But they
pale in comparison to my need for salvation. Thank You for
sending Your Son to shed His blood for my eternal need.

Do Not Pledge All of Your Assets

*Do not be a man who strikes hands in pledge or puts up security
for debts; if you lack the means to pay, your very bed will be
snatched from under you* (**Prov. 22:26-27**).

Suppose you and a friend decide to go into business together,
wholesaling clothing to department stores. You will handle sales,
and your partner will administer the office and warehouse and do
the bookkeeping. It will take about $100,000 to get off the ground,
including inventory, vehicle, and working capital. You have $20,000
in savings, and your friend can put up $10,000. The bank will lend
you $70,000 in a line of credit.

As collateral, the bank wants full security of equipment,
inventory, and receivables. Additionally, they get separate guaran-
tees—personal liability—from the partners. They stand to get all
of your assets in the event you default on the loan.

The business is a success right from the start, thanks to your
sales efforts. Then one day you come in and find a note from your
partner saying she had to leave town. She leaves no forwarding
address. The bank account is empty, the line of credit is drawn
down to zero, and you owe for orders to manufacturers totalling
tens of thousands of dollars. Your "partner" has turned her
$10,000 into $150,000, and left you holding the bag.

The bank seizes all of the collateral and you are out of business.
Then, in payment of the $50,000 still owing, they take your car,
your savings and securities, and finally your home and the very bed
in which you used to sleep at night. Through no fault of yours you
have lost all you own, and you and your family are left bankrupt.

This story is not far-fetched. It happens all of the time. People
sign personally on notes, only to find creditors knocking on the
door when a partner defaults. Noted writer on Proverbs, Derek
Kidner, says that these warnings against pledging assets do not
banish generosity, but rather gambling. Be careful. More than a
good night's sleep is at stake.

Prayer of Application

Dear Father, help me to avoid the traps that set themselves up
for the unwary. I know that indebtedness is one such trap,
particularly in guaranteeing indebtedness for another.

Discern Between Grace and Mercy

He who puts up security for another will surely suffer, but whoever refuses to strike hands in pledge is safe (Prov. 11:15).

God calls every Christian to be a vessel of mercy and kindness (Matt. 9:13; 18:32; 23:23). But we need to see the limits of mercy. Nowhere in Scripture are we called upon to go into debt for another person, in particular for strangers. Why? Because we do not know what the future holds. We may get ourselves and our families into trouble in a way that is not pleasing to God. Surely we are called to suffer for Christ (1 Pet. 1:21), but not in this way.

God is omniscient and knows all things, even our very thoughts. Furthermore, His omnipotence puts Him in control of all things. Because of his infinite wisdom and power, only God can be the fountainhead of grace. Grace goes above and beyond what mercy requires. While we may administer God's grace (1 Pet. 4:10), grace flows only from Him.

Therefore, if a stranger, or a friend, comes to you and asks you to co-sign a loan, don't do it. If your finances allow you to lend the person the money—and you can afford to lose it—go ahead and make the loan, or simply give the person the money. But God never calls us to take on unreasonable debt, and even commands us here *not* to do it.

Scriptural Examples

Judah. Joseph instructed his brothers not to return to Egypt unless they brought Benjamin (Gen. 42:19-20). Later, when their grain was gone, Jacob would not send their younger brother. But Judah uttered an oath of suretyship to his father, guaranteeing Benjamin's safety (Gen. 43:8-9). He put himself and his family at significant risk.

Jesus. Jesus was surety for others and is the human exception to the rule. As God, He redeemed strangers by taking our debts upon Him and suffering for us (Gal. 3:13).

Prayer of Application

Father, help me to understand that you want me to practice mercy, but that there is a limit to my resources and knowledge. Help me to know my limitations and not put my family at risk.

Understand the Source of All Wealth

The blessing of the Lord brings wealth, and he adds no trouble to it
(Prov. 10:22).

Proverbs 10:4 says that the hands of the diligent bring wealth. Here we're told that wealth comes from the Lord. Which is true? They both are. It is the combination of man's diligence, which is from God, and God's blessing. The slothful person seeks wealth without diligence. The practical atheist seeks wealth through her own diligence. But God distributes wealth as He sees fit.

Bob's friend Walt Henrichsen once startled a group of businessmen by saying, "There is no correlation between how hard a person works, and how much money that person earns." His statement went against everything the men had ever learned in the secular world about wealth creation.

But the woman who understands that God is the true source of wealth has a humble dependence upon her Source and a call to diligence that leaves the results to God. She will understand that riches are used as a blessing for one's family and for kingdom work and not for vain exercises of egotism. Such riches will bring blessing.

But for the slothful woman who wins the state lottery, or the diligent atheist who strikes it rich, wealth can bring trouble in spades and is worthless compared to the incalculable riches of knowing the One from whom it comes (Jer. 9:23-24).

Scriptural Examples

Job. His story makes it clear that it is God who bestows the blessing of wealth. Job's riches were from God, who took them all away, and then restored them two-fold (Job 1:10; 42:12).

The rich young ruler. This young man asked Jesus, "What must I do to inherit eternal life?" Seeing his covetousness, Jesus told him to give all his "wealth" away. The young man didn't realize that he was talking face-to-face with the One who had given him his riches in the first place (Matt. 19:16-22).

Prayer of Application

Sovereign God, You are the source of all blessing. Help me to use the blessings you provide as a blessing to others, as I provide for my family and for those who lack this world's goods.

Study Questions and Projects

1) Read Proverbs 10:22. Who brings wealth ultimately? How does the Lord's wealth differ from that of the wicked, according to Solomon? Have you known anyone who experienced sorrow as a result of wealth? Can you imagine different ways wealth could lead to sorrow?

2) Read Proverbs 23:4-5. What secret to wealth is given here? What warning?

3) In Proverbs 30:7-9, Agur makes two requests of God. What are they? What explanation does he give in verse 9 for his second request? Is this a prayer that makes sense for you and me? Why or why not? Discuss with others.

4) Read Matthew 13:22. In what way does Jesus say riches can be a real curse?

5) Jesus gives us another warning in Luke 12:15. What is it? To which of the Ten Commandments does He refer? Paul refers to the same sin in Colossians 3:5. To what does he compare it? Which of the Ten Commandments speak to that sin?

6) As a practical exercise, discuss with your group these issues:
    a) Is all wealth sinful? Is it wrong to be rich?
    b) What are some practical ways that we as women can ensure our families are saving enough for the future

Other Verses to Study
Deuteronomy 8:10-18; Isaiah 5:8; Matthew 6:19-20; 1 John 3:17.

One to Memorize
Finish your outdoor work and get your fields ready; after that, build your house (Prov. 24:27).

My Personal Action Plan to Be a Woman of Financial Wisdom

1) _____ 2) _____

3) _____ 4) _____

- Proverbs 31:17 -
She sets about her work vigorously;
her arms are strong for her tasks.

Chapter Nine

A Woman of Strength
• •

Paul says in Ephesians 6:10, "Be strong in the Lord and in his mighty power." Notice that Paul does not call on us to be strong in our own strength. We are to be "strong *in the Lord* and in *his* mighty power."

The most popular books in secular circles these days are "self-help" books. We humans are always looking for a quick fix, a way to find "inner strength" and to "tap the power within" us. The New Age movement, a reprise of the gnostic heresy of New Testament days, is providing much of this error. The truth is that *no* creature has power within itself. The only "power" we have has been given us by God. As Paul says of all people in Acts 17:28, "In [Christ] we live and move and have our being."

Today, much of what passes for Christian teaching is centered not on God, but on human beings, attributing much to the creature. But God is *all*-powerful. That means He has *all* the power. What little we have is given to us by Him. The Christian has the all-powerful God as her king and as her friend. We avail ourselves of God's strength and power through faith in Christ. And we rejoice in His mighty hand upon us.

Let us like Paul say that we delight in our weakness. "For when I am weak, then I am strong" (2 Cor. 12:9-10).

Walk by Faith in the Strength of the Lord

The way of the Lord is a refuge for the righteous, but it is the ruin of those who do evil. The righteous will never be uprooted, but the wicked will not remain in the land (Prov. 10:29-30).

The KJV renders "refuge" here as "strength," from a term some commentators translate "stronghold." But, of course, the Lord is all of these things. As the psalmist wrote in Psalm 46:1, "God is our refuge *and* strength, a very present help in trouble"(KJV).

What is the *way* of the Lord? It is the path of righteousness upon which each saved person should have her feet firmly planted (Jer. 6:16). But it is an alien way to us, and to attempt to walk it in our own strength is futile. Only God can supply the means to keep His way (2 Sam. 22:33-34).

And how are we to gain this strength? It is only through faith in the One who says He will give it to us (Eph. 1:18-20; Phil. 4:13). We need to walk daily by faith, trusting in the One who can deliver us from evil. We need to be rooted and grounded in the Lord Jesus and His Holy Word. The non-Christian does not even *see* her need for strengthening, because there is no conflict between evil and righteousness within her. Apart from Christ, no one is righteous.

Scriptural Examples

Joshua. God ordered him to be "strong and courageous" and gave him a recipe for such strength. He was to obey the law of Moses, to meditate upon it day and night, and then to trust in the Lord his God who would be with him always (Josh. 1:6-9).

Babylon and Tyre. These ancient cities typify the wicked who think they have strongholds in their earthly wealth and power. It was only a matter of time before they met ruin and destruction. Their "strength" was a sham (Jer. 51:49-54; Zech. 9:3-4).

The Old Testament saints. These people accomplished all sorts of incredible things because "through faith" their "weakness was turned to strength" (Heb. 11:32-34).

Prayer of Application

Sovereign God, teach me Your ways and strengthen me in the path of righteousness. Increase my faith in Your Word and in You, that I may find Your strength for my every need.

Be Strengthened by the Indwelling Spirit

*A man's spirit sustains him in sickness, but a crushed
spirit who can bear?* (Prov. 18:14).

A woman's strength of spirit in infirmity is often amazing. Acts
of heroism, stoicism in the face of poverty, a resignation to pain and
sickness—all of these speak to the strength that God puts in us. But
human strength only goes so far. The Christian woman has far
greater resources. A crushed spirit may sink the non-Christian, but
the Christian has hope in the midst of dire affliction.

In today's world, many women suffer from depression, guilt, or
shame. While the counsel of secular psychiatrists may provide a
temporary cure at best, they do not diagnose the real root of the
problem: sin. The spiritual woman has Christ's strengthening Spirit
within her (Eph. 3:16). That doesn't mean she can't benefit from
Christian counselors, but it's the Holy Spirit who heals her crushed
spirit. God takes us to the cross, where we see ourselves as we really
are, sinners in need of a Savior. There, by God's grace, while we were
His enemies, Christ died for us (Eph. 2:5). Christ alone is the cure
for the crushed spirit. Go to Him and be healed (Isa. 53:5).

Scriptural Examples

Job. In the midst of infirmity, Job still praised God. God
allowed Satan to crush Job's spirit until he cursed the day of his
birth. Later, Job had a renewed hope in God, saying, "Though he
slay me, yet will I hope in him" (Job 13:15; see also 1:21; 3:1).

Mary. In her song to God, Mary spoke of His strengthening
Spirit. She sang, "He has brought down rulers from their thrones,
but has lifted up the humble. He has filled the hungry with good
things but has sent the rich away empty" (Luke 1:52-53).

The martyrs. These men and women down through the ages
have found peace in the arms of Christ and the hope they had in
Him. They were more than conquerers (Rom. 8:37) because of His
Spirit that was within them (Heb. 11:35-39).

Prayer of Application

Heavenly Father, thank You for Your Holy Spirit. Even
though I may face a crushed spirit which sinks me to the depths of
mourning, I will not fear, for He will uplift me even then.

Find Strength in the Lord Your Refuge

*He who fears the Lord has a secure fortress, and for his
children it will be a refuge* (Prov. 14:26).

How can "fear" and "security" operate together? We usually
think of them as opposites. Here, however, we are told that the fear
of the Lord leads to the security of a fortress. The answer lies in our
understanding of the phrase "the fear of the Lord." This is not the
fear that perfect love casts out (1 John 4:18), but the fear that love
brings in. It is the reverence that a child has for his or her parents,
and that prompts the child to obey them regardless of the circumstances. Fear of the Lord is taking delight in what God commands
us to do (Ps. 112:1).We *fear* the Lord, but we're not *afraid* of the
Lord. Our fear of Him gives us boldness and strength, strong
confidence and security. We find such confidence in bold and
faithful prayer.

But how does this provide a refuge for our children? Not only
are they protected by the umbrella of God's covenant with their
saved parent(s) (1 Cor. 7:14), but when they see what we do—
taking refuge in the Lord—they will learn our source of strength.

Scriptural Examples

Abraham. When God commanded Abraham to take Isaac to
Mt. Moriah and offer him as a sacrifice, the two set out in fear, yet
in faith. Abraham, in his fear of God, knew that even if he was
required to sacrifice Isaac, God had the power to raise his son from
the dead (Gen. 22:2-14; Heb.11:17-19).

Nehemiah. As he prepared the people for the Sabbath, the day
that was sacred to their Lord, he encouraged them, saying, "Do not
grieve, for the joy of the Lord is your strength" (Neh. 8:10).

Stephen. As the Sanhedrin began to stone him, Stephen
looked to heaven and saw his refuge opened before him. He
expressed confidence in his heavenly advocate Jesus, whom he saw
standing at the right hand of the Father (Acts 7:55-60).

Prayer of Application

Father, I thank You that because of Jesus' finished work on the
cross, where He reconciled me to You, I have found refuge from
my fear of death. Help me to find a daily refuge in You.

Get Christ: Let Him Guard Your Life

*Above all else, guard your heart, for it is the wellspring of life.
Put away perversity from your mouth; keep corrupt talk far from
your lips. Let your eyes look straight ahead, fix your gaze directly
before you. Make level paths for your feet and take only ways that
are firm. Do not swerve to the right or the left; keep
your foot from evil* (**Prov.** 4:23-27).

In the seventeenth century, William Harvey discovered the importance of the heart in the circulation of blood. But long before Harvey's day, God spoke of the spiritual heart of a person: the seat of the human personality, character, and will— "the wellspring of life." Before the new birth, our hearts are exceedingly wicked and deceitful (Jer. 17:9; Matt. 15:19). No one seeks God unless a new heart is given by His Spirit (John 3:3).

At salvation, a struggle begins between the believer's heart and the sin nature that remains in her. She discovers that she has no power to walk in newness of life, so that all her ways are righteous (Rom. 7:19). She finds that only by submitting her heart to Christ can she have any success at all (Rom. 7:20-24; 1 Pet. 4:19).

Notice that the heart is not the only body part of which these proverbs speak. There are also lips, mouth, eyes, and feet. If the water from the wellspring is polluted, so, too, will be a person's words, that which her eyes drink in, and the paths down which she walks. We need to keep our eyes fixed on the One who can keep our whole body full of light (Matt. 6:22).

Scriptural Examples

Eve. Eve gazed upon the fruit and lusted after it with her mouth, with her eyes, and finally with her heart (Gen. 3:6).

Job. This righteous man made a covenant with his eyes, that he would not look lustfully at a girl (Job 31:1; Matt 5:28).

Mary Magdalene. This woman was marvelously saved from evil spirits. Out of her new heart came strength (Luke 8:2-3).

Prayer of Application

Sovereign God, I am powerless to keep Your commands without Your Spirit working in and through Your Word. Help me to submit fully to the power of the Spirit and the Word.

Find Wisdom's Ultimate Protection

For wisdom will enter your heart, and knowledge will be pleasant to your soul. Discretion will protect you, and understanding will guard you (**Prov. 2:10-11**).

Our diligence brings knowledge when we mine the Word of God for wisdom. But you will notice that verse 10 says "…wisdom will enter your *heart,* and knowledge will be pleasant to your soul." This is the work that God's grace does, and it makes all the difference. For it is out of a woman's *heart* that the issues of life come (Prov. 4:23; Matt.15:19).

And what are these "issues of life"? Some years ago, comedians Mel Brooks and Carl Reiner did a skit called "The 2,000 Year Old Man." When (milligenarian)Mel was asked what motivated men 2,000 years ago, he replied, "Fear, mostly." For the unsaved woman, the fearsome issue of life is *protection.* That is one reason she seeks earthly wealth, job security, health foods and the like, because she fears poverty, death, sickness, and so forth.

But the Bible tells us that "perfect love drives out fear" (1 John 4:18). The Christian woman is to be motivated by this perfect love that God's grace has put into her quickened heart (Ezek. 11:19-20). This perfect love seeks to glorify God, to love Him with all of one's heart, soul, strength, and mind (Deut 6:5; Luke 10:27). She seeks also to love her neighbor even as she loves herself. The joy and love of Christ frees us to be the kind of people God wants us to be.

Scriptural Examples

Habakkuk. Amy's favorite verses in the Bible are these from Habakkuk 3:17-19: "Though the fig tree does not bud and there are no grapes on the vines, though the olive crop fails and the fields produce no food, though there are no sheep in the pen and no cattle in the stalls, yet I will rejoice in the Lord, I will be joyful in God my Savior. The Sovereign Lord is my strength; he makes my feet like the feet of a deer, he enables me to go on the heights."

Prayer of Application

Heavenly Father, thank You for Your protecting fence about me. Even though I walk through the valley of the shadow of death, Your rod and Your staff will protect me forever.

Sisters, Disciple One Another

As iron sharpens iron, so one man sharpens another
(Prov. 27:17).

One good way to build strength in the Lord is to cultivate a discipling relationship with another Christian. As we share our joys, our troubles, and our heartaches with each other, and as we share newfound insights from the Word, we can see first-hand how the Lord is working to protect us and provide for us. Teaching and encouraging one another is foundational in the Christian life (Col. 3:16; 1 Thess. 5:11).

The Christian life needs to be lived in intimate fellowship with others who share our precious faith. The writer to the Hebrews enjoins us to "encourage one another daily," to the end that "none of you may be hardened by sin's deceitfulness" (Heb. 3:13). This can be done neither in the context of a "loner" mentality nor that of a very large group. There has to be personal intimacy, and this is only possible in the small group or one-on-one discipling relationships.

If you are not involved in a small women's group or discipling ministry of some kind, we urge you to get involved. The only requirement is to be serious about living for and glorifying the Lord Jesus, and a consequent desire to be sharpened in your walk with God, and to sharpen others.

Scriptural Examples

Job. Eliphaz the Temanite spoke of his friend Job's discipling ministry. Job's words had supported those who had stumbled, and had strengthened those who had faltering knees (Job 4:3-4).

The men on the Emmaus Road. After the crucifixion, two men were walking from Jerusalem to Emmaus when a stranger appeared and spoke to them about the prophecies that had been fulfilled in Christ. Later, they recognized the stranger as the Lord Jesus, who had just discipled them (Luke 24:13ff).

Prayer of Application

Father God, thank You for my brothers and sisters in Christ, who share common experiences on the road of faith. Help me to take seriously my responsibility to encourage and disciple others.

Study Questions and Projects

1) The 23rd Psalm is a favorite of everyone. Using your own words, rewrite each phrase given. It may be helpful to discuss the exercise with friends. You will need to use additional paper.

   a) The Lord is my shepherd –

   b) I shall not be in want –

   c) He makes me lie down in green pastures –

   d) He leads me beside quiet waters –

   e) He restores my soul –

   f) He guides me in paths of righteousness –

   g) For his name's sake –

   h) Even though I walk through the valley of the shadow of death I will fear no evil –

   i) For you are with me –

   j) Your rod and your staff they comfort me –

   k) You prepare a table before me –

   l) In the presence of my enemies –

   m) You anoint my head with oil –

   n) My cup overflows –

   o) Surely goodness and love will follow me all the days of my life –

   p) And I will dwell in the house of the Lord forever –

Other Verses to Study
Exodus 15:2; Psalms 28:7 and 59:9, 17;
1 Corinthians 16:13; Hebrews 1:3.

One to Memorize
He who fears the Lord has a secure fortress, and for his children it will be a refuge (Prov. 14:26).

My Personal Action Plan to Be a Woman of Strength

1) _____ 2) _____

3) _____ 4) _____

- Proverbs 31:18 -
She sees that her trading is profitable,
and her lamp does not go out at night.

Chapter Ten

A Woman of Commerce

The Bible's principles of commerce apply to all callings, whether your business is in the marketplace, the office, or the home. One principle stated in Proverbs 31:18 is that of profit. The woman's trading is "always profitable." Some have the idea that "profit" is a bad word, that it's somehow wrong in God's view. But nothing could be further from the truth. Every thing we do entails the concept of profitability. The concept of the hope for profit doesn't arise from our sin nature; it's the way God has created us.

Think about it. Almost every choice we make is according to what we perceive to be most profitable at the time. The last time you bought a pair of shoes, you figured that it was more profitable for you to have the shoes than it was to have the money you paid for them. Jesus, in the parable of the talents (Matt. 25:14-30), expected the master's servants to invest and make a profit. The servant that failed to even try was cast out into the darkness.

It's what we do with our profits that counts. And, to be sure, the Bible condemns someone who profits excessively at the expense of others. In the verses to follow, the proverbs give us some varied guidelines as to how to maximize our profitability, while at the same time maximizing God's glory.

Practice Absolute Honesty

Differing weights and differing measures—the Lord detests them both (**Prov. 20:10**).

If a person owns a grocery store and permits its produce scales to weigh just a slight bit heavy, so that for every true pound of potatoes she is charging for 1.02 pounds, then she has stolen from her customer just as certainly as if she had pilfered the stereo from her customer's car. Actually, what the grocerywoman has done may be worse than common burglary, because she has done it in the context of a seemingly honest business transaction in which an innocent party is tricked.

We Christians must practice squeaky-clean honesty in all our dealings. We must do this not just because we know that our God is omniscient, and that His judgment is like a consuming fire (Heb. 12:29). We are to do it primarily out of love for Christ, and a desire to see His name glorified in us.

Scriptural Examples

Delilah. She was the world's first female double agent. While pretending to love Samson and to be committed to his welfare, she teamed up with the rulers of the Philistines to take away his God-given superhuman powers. She finally succeeded in her trickery as Samson revealed his long hair to be the key (Judg. 16:4-21).

Satan. Called "the king of Tyre," it is nevertheless Satan who is described by Ezekiel. At one time a blameless and beautiful creature, Satan's heart became proud and he engaged in sins and dishonest trade. Satan is the father of lies (John 8:44), and the father of dishonest scales, too (Ezek. 28:12-19).

Judas. Judas complained that the perfume lavished upon Jesus by Martha's sister Mary was a waste. He said its value could have been given to the poor. But Judas didn't care about the poor. He was a dishonest schemer, who would probably have kept the money for himself (John 12:4-6).

Prayer of Application

Lord, every day I run into situations where my honesty is tested. It may be in financial matters, in my relationships, or in my work. Help me, Lord, to be honest always and to glorify You.

Be a Distributor, Not an Accumulator

He who increases his wealth by exorbitant interest amasses it for another, who will be kind to the poor (**Prov. 28:8**).

The law of Moses let the Israelites charge interest to foreigners, but not to brothers (Deut. 23:19-20). As Derek Kidner points out, the Hebrews were a family. Charging interest would be the same as a physician charging his own children for care (*Proverbs*, p. 170).

But this proverb speaks to more than just the sin of usury. The KJV renders the first line, "He that by usury *and unjust gain* increaseth his substance...." The idea is that any unjust means of accumulating wealth brings judgment. We in business need to be especially watchful. Are we willing to cheat just a little bit in order to improve quarterly profits? If we do, God will pass on our ill-gotten gains to someone who will be kind to the poor.

Material wealth brings with it increased responsibility and accountability. To whom much is given will much be required, as we know from Luke 12:48. God will call us to account for what we did with the resources He gave us. Therefore, we Christians should not be in the accumulation business, but in the distribution business, distributing the Gospel, our knowledge, encouragement, gifts, joy, and our material wealth to everyone in need.

Scriptural Examples

Jezebel. This woman's name has come down through history as synonymous with evil. She was definitely an accumulator, not a distributor. A foreigner married to Israel's King Ahab, she conspired with her spouse to rob Naboth the Jezreelite of his vineyard *and* his life. The wicked pair had Naboth falsely charged with cursing God and the king, and had him stoned to death. Their treachery did not go unnoticed by God (1 Kings 21:1-19).

The Jewish brothers. The pilgrims sent up a loud cry against their brothers who had been illegally charging them interest during times of famine and excessive taxation (Neh. 5:1-13).

Prayer of Application

Lord, help me to understand that true wealth is in trusting You. May I be a distributor of Your wealth, forsaking usury and unjust gain, and clinging rather to justice and equity.

Do Your Work as Unto the Lord

He who tends a fig tree will eat its fruit, and he who looks after his master will be honored (Prov. 27:18).

Back in Bob's college summers he worked as either a laborer or carpenter. His dad would say to him as he left for work, "Make a profit for your employer today." Bob found that he meant if his hard work made a profit for his employer, he'd make a profit, too.

The wise employee who tends to his employer's needs will himself be honored and enriched. At least that's the way it is supposed to work. Books could be filled with tales of unscrupulous employers who failed to pay the worker's wages or who absconded with the company pension funds.

As Christians, we need to understand that it is our heavenly Father who signs our paychecks. Everything we have, or ever will have, comes from His hand. Somehow, we have lost confidence in the providence of God over all of our affairs. But that doesn't make it less true. God is in control of all events.

What it boils down to is this: If you are seeking justice in the work you perform every day in your employer's service, or even working for yourself, look to the One True Employer to provide it (Col. 3:22-24). We seek honor from our heavenly master.

Scriptural Examples

The faithful servants. In this story, Jesus illustrates the rewards given out in the kingdom of heaven to those who have been good and faithful servants. We need to work for the reward that never perishes, laboring in the field of the Lord for His glory and profit, and for our eternal joy (Matt. 25:14-23).

The fig tree. In order for a fruit tree to bear fruit, it needs attention. Jesus spoke of a man telling his servant to cut down an unproductive fig tree. The man begged to be allowed to dig around the tree and fertilize it. The owner honored his servant's wish and gave the tree one more chance (Luke 13:6-10).

Prayer of Application

Oh, Father, whatever I do, help me to do it unto You and for Your glory. Lord, I thank You that every calling is a sacred calling, and all labor has its focus in Your honor and glory.

Prefer Integrity to Riches

*Better a poor man whose walk is blameless than a fool
whose lips are perverse* (Prov. 19:1).

In business as in life, a person is often faced with difficult
decisions. For instance, suppose you found out that the company
you manage uses a particular software program on ten computers,
but has only purchased licenses for four. The chances that you will
be discovered for this copyright infringement are slim indeed, and
it will cost $2,100 to purchase the other six, which in turn will
adversely affect the bottom line. What do you do? This proverb
gives you the answer. Spend the money and let the bottom line
suffer. Don't forfeit principle for pragmatism.

The outward show of wealth is honored more in our society
than is the hidden heart of integrity. That's one reason why fancy
cars and big homes are popular. There's nothing wrong in owning
a fancy car or a big home, but in God's economy, the heart of
integrity is worth much more. What good is it for a woman to be rich
in the world's things, but poor in the things of God? (Luke 12:21).

Scriptural Examples

Joseph and Potiphar's wife. What may have been viewed by
some slaves as an opportunity for personal advancement, Joseph
fled with his integrity intact (Gen. 39:8-12).

Shiprah, Puah, and Pharaoh. The midwives feared God more
than they feared the perverse king, and refused to commit sin by
killing the newborn Hebrew boys (Ex. 1:15-19).

Peter and Simon Magus. Peter, in his integrity, rebuked
Simon and his money, and called upon him to repent of the
perverseness and sin in his heart (Acts 8:18-23).

Paul, Barnabas, and the Lycaonians. In Lystra, Paul healed a
man who had never walked. The people called Paul and Barnabas
"Hermes" and "Zeus," and proceeded to worship them. But the
apostles would have none of it (Acts 14:8-15).

Prayer of Application

Father, sensitize my heart to keep Your commandments. Point
out areas in my life that may deviate even slightly from truth and
justice, or even the smallest breach of integrity.

Interview Prospective Employees Carefully

*Like an archer who wounds at random is he who hires a
fool or any passer-by* (Prov. 26:10).

If you are ever placed in a position where it is your responsibility to hire new employees, approach that task with all the diligence you can muster. It is most critical in any business and can literally mean the difference between success or failure. Just to pick the first person who walks in the door, whether the job is for janitor or chief executive officer, is like walking in front of a machine gun nest. It is fraught with peril. And in today's society of frivolous lawsuits and fraudulent claims, it's even more critical than when this proverb was written.

Bob once had a very good employee quit. She had been the receptionist, secretary, accounts receivable and payable clerk, and bookkeeper, all rolled into one. He was in a panic to hire someone to fill her shoes, so he interviewed a few people and then chose a woman he hoped would fit. It didn't take long to find out that she was a disaster. Her foul language and rough manner alienated both customers and other employees alike. Bob was thankful that she did not sue the company upon her termination.

Almost every month or so we hear of a gunman who opens fire in a crowded subway, on a college campus, or in a restaurant. This proverb compares that gunman with the hiring of a "fool or any passer-by." Be selective in your hiring. Remember that the prospective employee will never look better than during the interview. Get the opinion of others and take your time.

Scriptural Examples

The vineyard laborers. Jesus likened the kingdom of heaven to a landowner who hired laborers. He didn't interview them, he just called them in. Careful study reveals that the landowner was God, and He doesn't need to interview. He's omniscient. We are not omniscient! Interview carefully! (Matt. 20:1-16).

Prayer of Application

Father, thank You for the responsibility of choosing others as employees. But I cannot always see through the smile and the resume. Help me to choose those who will succeed.

Manage Expectations and Entitlements

If a man pampers his servant from youth, he will bring grief in the end (**Prov. 29:21**).

In 1981 Bob started a company which grew rapidly in seven years. During that time, he sometimes made the error of promising his employees more than he could deliver. He didn't do it deceitfully, or to manipulate them. He was naïvely optimistic. But whether the promises were fulfilled or not isn't the point. Bob believes he should have managed expectations more carefully.

If an employee, or a family member, is allowed to have her expectations grow beyond reality, you are sure to get grief when disappointments come. When tough times hit, morale goes south. How much better to manage the expectations of those under your authority. Then when those tough times come, they are more acclimated to taking their lumps with you. When times get better, that fat bonus comes as a welcome surprise.

A regular gift to someone, even though done out of kindness, may quickly become in her eyes an entitlement. If the gift is then withheld in the future, its withdrawal becomes an injustice. Also, if you pamper your employee, or your child, and never hold her accountable, she will begin to expect the same in the future. The point is that we need to be careful in raising the expectations of others, because they will come to view our hopeful promises or current treatment of them as an entitlement.

How do we avoid this trap? The best way is to set goals and put them in writing. Hold everyone who is looking to you for leadership accountable for their actions, whether they are an employee or your child. Make sure that everyone understands that this year's bonus is given only because the company made certain financial goals, or the family was able to save beyond its expectations. Tell them not to expect it next year. In other words, condition others to expect reality and they won't be disappointed and give you grief when their false hopes are dashed.

Prayer of Application

Dear Father, thank You for Your many precious promises. You will never fail us. But help those of us in authority to help others see reality in their expectations of You and of us.

Study Questions and Projects

1) Read Leviticus 19:36-37. What laws does God give the Israelites which will govern their business activities? To which verse in Proverbs do these precepts relate?

2) Read Leviticus 25:14-17. What matters of Hebrew real estate law are given here? (For a description of the Jubilee and all that it entailed, read all of chapter 25.) Why do you suppose God considered these laws fair for both parties to the land sale?

3) Read Revelation 18:2-4. What sin related to business and commerce does John see in mighty Babylon the Great? What advice does the voice from heaven give us in verse 4?

4) What do the merchants in Nahum 3:16 do that is so bad? Do you see that kind of sin happening in the world today?

5) Turn to the book of James in the New Testament.

   a) Read 3:16. What two sins are mentioned here? What are their results in society? How prevalent do you think these sins are in America's business community today? Discuss with others.

   b) James 4:13-17 is also about commerce. What is it that these businesspeople are doing that is so terrible? How clear of a picture do you have of the providence of God for your life? Do you think these people trusted God for their provision or themselves?

Other Verses to Study
Proverbs 6:6-11; 14:4; 16:26; 18:9; 20:13; 22:29.

One to Memorize
Differing weights and differing measures—the Lord detests them both (Prov. 20:10).

My Personal Action Plan to Be a Woman of Commerce

1) _____ 2) _____

3) _____ 4) _____

- Proverbs 31:19 -
In her hand she holds the distaff
and grasps the spindle with her fingers.

Chapter Eleven

A Woman of Humility

•••••••••••••••••••••••••••••••

This entrepreneurial businesswoman of Proverbs 31 is a humble woman. Yes, she trades farmland and is a successful merchant, but she's not above working humbly with her hands at the spinning wheel or weaver's loom. As we shall see in the next chapter, her humility extends to all other areas of her life as well.

St. Augustine said that the Christian life could be described in three words: "Humility, humility, and humility." Humility should characterize the life of the Christian just as it characterized the life of our Lord. He said in Matthew 11:29, "Take my yoke upon you and learn from me, for I am gentle and humble in heart, and you will find rest for your souls." And then in Matthew 20:26, "Whoever wants to become great among you must be your servant, and whoever wants to be first must be your slave."

John said, "Whoever claims to live in [Christ] must walk as Jesus did" (1 John 2:6). How did Jesus walk? Philippians 2:6-7 says of Jesus, "Being in very nature God, [He] did not consider equality with God something to be grasped, but made himself nothing, [and] taking the very nature of a servant, being made in human likeness." Christ's humility exceeds our comprehension. He calls those who follow Him to humbly obey Him and give our lives for others.

Humble Yourself in the Sight of the Lord

The fear of the Lord teaches a man wisdom, and humility comes before honor (**Prov. 15:33**).

One scriptural example of this principle stands far above the rest. Our Savior, exalted in heaven as the Great and Mighty God, Creator and Sustainer of the universe, humbled Himself to the state of a common human child and died a criminal's death in order that we might be exalted. Although his self-humiliation was far greater than we can even imagine, we are to have this same mind that was in Christ (Phil. 2:5), and to humble ourselves in the sight of the Lord (James 4:10).

"The fear of the Lord" speaks of the reverent awe in which we are to hold our God. Humility is seeing ourselves as we really are, warts and all. This is the instruction of wisdom. It begins with submitting to His gospel, knowing that there is nothing in and of ourselves that recommends us to Him. It continues with submission to the authority of His Word, the application of which sanctifies us. In the end, when we leave the earth, we will be exalted with our Savior, joint heirs with Him of the eternal treasures of God. Unthinkable! Unimaginable! But true!

Scriptural Examples

Gideon. The son of a prostitute, he described himself as "the least of the families of Israel." But God lifted this man up to be judge and leader of His people Israel (Judg. 6–8).

The woman accused of adultery. She is a picture of all humans. She was accused by the Pharisees who wanted her stoned to death. But Jesus wrote something in the sand. It might have been sins that each of her accusers had committed, because they left one by one. Jesus said to her, "Has no one condemned you? . . .Neither do I condemn you . . . Go and leave your life of sin." In the same way, Christ elevates those who will admit they stand condemned before Him (John 8:1-11).

Prayer of Application

Dear God, help me to see myself by the light of Your Word, that I might be humbled in Your eternal wisdom. How I look forward to that day when I shall see my Lord face to face.

Beware of Pride that Goes Before a Fall

Before his downfall a man's heart is proud, but humility comes before honor (**Prov. 18:12**).

Bob's personal testimony speaks to the verse above: "When I was saved in 1971, I was with a large commercial real estate brokerage firm. In 1972, I decided to leave that organization and start my own development company. God had been 'real smart' to save me, and I was going to 'cut a wide swath' for Him, making lots of money for His kingdom. My real motives, of course, were to pridefully create a name for myself and to live a life of luxury.

"Three years later, I owed more money than I ever could hope to repay. I moved my family to Florida in order to earn a living. There, for the next six years, God continued to humble me. Returning to San Diego, I started a business in 1981 with only an idea, and virtually no money. God has prospered that company, and has allowed me to pay off my development debts.

"No longer does honor from men appeal to me. I have learned much in the school of God's discipline, the most important lesson being that one should live his life for God alone. If the Lord God wants to honor me, that's His business. My business is to humbly obey Him."

Scriptural Examples

Moses. We are told in Numbers 12:3 that Moses was a very humble man, more so than any man who was on the earth. God lifted him up in high honor in the midst of his meekness.

Uzziah. This king of Judah became very prideful. He entered the temple to burn incense to the Lord, an activity only allowed the priests, and God struck him with leprosy. He carried that disease until the day he died (2 Chron. 26:16-21).

Satan. Described in Ezekiel as the "king of Tyre," Satan is said to have become proud of his beauty, and so his wisdom was corrupted. God threw him out of heaven (Ezek. 28:17).

Prayer of Application

Heavenly Father, search my heart for the pride that clings so deep and remove it from me. Place in me a humble spirit that I might only boast in You, and of Your grace and providence.

Imitate the Humility of Christ

Do not exalt yourself in the king's presence, and do not claim a place among great men; it is better for him to say to you, "Come up here," than for him to humiliate you before a nobleman (**Prov. 25:6-7**).

God chose to reveal Himself to us in His Son, "who being in very nature God, did not consider equality with God something to be grasped, but made himself nothing, taking the very nature of a servant, being made in human likeness. And being found in appearance as a man, he humbled himself and became obedient unto death, even death on a cross" (Phil. 2:6-8).

A wonderful old hymn includes the line: "Out of the ivory palaces, into a world of woe." The song tells the story of Jesus, who in unfathomable humility, came to this earth to die for the sins of people like you and me. In doing so, He revealed God's character of ultimate humility, grace, and love.

How much different we are. We prideful humans seek to elevate ourselves in the eyes of others and will use every trick in the book to do it. How foolish we are and what a glaring difference between our character and that of the Living God. Humble yourself after the example of Jesus.

Scriptural Examples

The disciples. They argued amongst themselves as to who was the greatest. They didn't get it, did they? Jesus said, "If anyone wants to be first, he must be last" (Mark 9:33-35).

The Roman centurion. He asked Jesus to heal his servant but said he didn't deserve Him under his roof. Jesus lauded his faith and appreciated his humility as well (Luke 7:2-10).

The party guest. Jesus attended a party once where guests sought places of honor, and told a parable about a man who didn't heed this proverb. He was humiliated when his host asked him to move to a lesser seat (Luke 14:7-10).

Prayer of Application

Dear God, how far I am from the excellence of your divine nature. I can taste it, but I can't duplicate it. Help me to grow more in the likeness of Your humble Son, and hence bring Him glory.

Humbly Practice Self-Control

Like a city whose walls are broken down is a man who
lacks self-control (Prov. 25:28).

In the ancient world and through the Middle Ages, cities were fortified with walls against the potential attack of invading armies. Sometimes other barriers such as moats and pits were also constructed, but the walls of a city were its ultimate protection. A breach in the city's walls during a battle meant disaster, as the invaders poured into the city.

We, too, have walls like those ancient cities, and enemies who seek to break through the weak spots and destroy us. How do we keep our walls from being breached? First, let's admit our weaknesses. Do a complete self-inventory just as Nehemiah inventoried the walls of Jerusalem that had been broken down (Neh. 2:3-5). Second, humbly submit to God's Spirit in prayer, asking for strength to reinforce those weaknesses (Matt. 26:41). Third, share your weaknesses with close friends, asking them for prayer and support. There is strength in humility and encouragement in numbers, particularly in times of temptation.

What are the results of the breach of a personal wall? A witness for Christ is limited or destroyed. A life of service is hobbled or even shut down. The joy of purity is extinguished in guilt and sadness. Families are broken apart. There is loss of heavenly reward (1 Cor. 9:27). Watch your walls with care and prayer. Humble yourself before the living God. A breach in the walls can be devastating.

Scriptural Examples

Paul. Paul boasted in his weaknesses. Why? Because he realized that it was through his weakness that the Lord's strength could be manifested. When he complained to God about a certain thorn in his flesh, the Lord said, "My grace is sufficient for you, for my power is made perfect in weakness." This same power is available to each of us if we humbly submit to it (2 Cor. 12:7-10).

Prayer of Application

Father, thank You for the power to live my life in a way that is pleasing to You. But I have weaknesses in my walls that need constant attention. Help me to be strong by relying on You only.

Be Willing to Be Wrong

*The way of a fool seems right to him, but a wise man
listens to advice* (Prov. 12:15).

Have you ever known a person who would not respond to
proof? Some refuse to acknowledge the facts because their minds
are already made up. Someone like this is puffed up in her view of
herself, and thinks that clear teaching is beneath her dignity to
consider. This verse says that such a person is a fool.

The visible church has its share of those who are not teachable.
They may know Christ as their Savior, and are therefore not fools
in the full sense of the word, but they cling to dogma that has no
scriptural basis. They refuse to change their position on some
matters and doggedly cling to their own ideas, even though valid
proof exists that refutes them. But Christ calls His followers to
humility and a teachable spirit (Matt. 18:3-4; 5:3). Be solidly
grounded in the Word, but also seek the input of godly men and
women, and of the Holy Spirit. Don't adopt every wind of
doctrine that comes down the pike, and be ready to change your
mind if necessary. In other words, be willing to be wrong.

Scriptural Examples

The rich young ruler. This man asked what he had to do to
inherit eternal life. When Jesus told him to keep the Law of Moses,
he responded that he had. But Jesus saw his covetousness. The
young man wouldn't be instructed in the truth (Matt. 19:16-22).

The prideful Pharisee. The Pharisee thanked God that he was
more righteous than others; that he observed the law in detail. The
tax collector just beat his breast and asked for mercy. Jesus said that
it was the latter who was justified before God (Luke 18:9-14).

Apollos. He was thoroughly trained in the Scriptures, but
knew only the baptism of John. Paul's friends, Priscilla and Aquila,
took him into their home and explained to him the gospel of Jesus
Christ. Apollos was teachable (Acts 18:24-26).

Prayer of Application

Dear Heavenly Father, thank You for Your Word and for its
counsel in my life. Keep me teachable, Lord, so that I don't become
wise in my own eyes and depart from Your truth.

Walk Humbly and Fear the Lord

Humility and the fear of the Lord bring wealth and honor and life
(**Prov. 22:4**).

Sit back for a few minutes with us and try to imagine what the perfect life would be like. What follows is an imaginary dialogue with someone who has done that.

"Okay, let's see. First, there would be lots of money. I could use it to help my church build that new building and to help missionaries and others on the Christian field. There's also that new home I've always wanted." What else? "Well, I'd like to have some recognition. I was never a raving beauty or super student and have never received much in the way of earthly honors." Okay, what else? "Well, I'd like a fulfilling life, an enriching and meaningful occupation, a life with a big family and lots of friends, filled with excitement and good health, with love and contentment."

Now open your eyes and let me tell you about a life that's *more* than all that. It is the Christian life, a life of *humility* and the *fear of the Lord.* Humility is coming to grips with who we really are—spiritually helpless and lost without Christ. We are not as bad as we could be, but only because of the restraining power of God's Spirit. Next, it is understanding that God is holy, righteous, just, omniscient, omnipresent, and omnipotent and yet loving and kind and merciful. Then, to realize how He has honored us through the Lord Jesus is to fall trembling at His feet in thanksgiving, joyfulness, adoration, and awe—the *fear of the Lord.*

Christians have riches beyond comprehension. Your heavenly Father knows your needs and has promised to provide all things richly to you for your benefit. Nothing will ever happen to you that will be "bad" in an eternal context (Rom. 8:28-32; Matt. 6:25-34; Phil. 4:19). You have riches that will endure (Rom. 8:17), never to spoil or be taken away (Matt. 6:20). You are part of the wonderful family of God. The Christian life of humility is a life that will surpass any of your wildest dreams.

Prayer of Application

Dear Lord, thank You for eternal life. Help me to see that that life began the moment I trusted You. Give me the strength to live it to the fullest now. Help me live humbly above my circumstances.

Study Questions and Projects

1) Compare Jesus' statement in Matthew 23:12 (or Luke 14:11) with Proverbs 18:12. Who does the honoring or exalting?

2) What principle of leadership does Jesus give us in John 13:14-16? How can you use what He says?

3) What principles of humility does Paul give us in these verses from his epistles? What application do they have to your life?

  a) Romans 12:3 – _____

_____

  b) Romans 12:10 – _____

_____

  c) Romans 12:16 – _____

_____

  d) 1 Corinthians 3:18 – _____

_____

  e) 1 Corinthians 10:12 – _____

_____

  g) Galatians 6:14 – _____

_____

  f) Ephesians 4:2 – _____

_____

Other Verses to Study
Deuteronomy 15:15; James 4:6, 10; 1 Peter 5:5-6.

One to Memorize
Before his downfall a man's heart is proud, but humility comes before honor (Prov. 18:12).

My Personal Action Plan to Be a Woman of Humility

1)_____ 2)_____

3)_____ 4)_____

- Proverbs 31:20 -
She opens her arms to the poor
and extends her hands to the needy.

Chapter Twelve

A Woman of Mercy

Jesus said in Luke 6:35-36, "But love your enemies, do good to them, and lend to them without expecting to get anything back. Then your reward will be great, and you will be sons of the Most High, because he is kind to the ungrateful and wicked. Be merciful, just as your Father is merciful."

Another verse that is one of our favorites in Scripture is from Micah 6:8. "He has showed you, O man, what is good. And what does the Lord require of you? To act justly and to *love mercy* and to walk humbly with your God." Mercy is closely connected to justice and humility in God's eyes. We humble ourselves with compassion for the poor and needy, providing for their needs as representatives of our God to them.

There are many ways in which we can show mercy. As you study, brainstorm with others some ways in which you can be more merciful to others, in thought, word, and deed. Mercy is a crucial aspect of our walk with Christ. He said of the sheep of His fold; "For I was hungry and you gave me something to eat, I was thirsty and you gave me something to drink, I was a stranger and you invited me in, I needed clothes and you clothed me, I was sick and you looked after me, I was in prison and you came to visit me… Whatever you did for [others], you did for me" (Matt. 25:35-40).

Invest in the Poor

He who is kind to the poor lends to the Lord, and he will reward him for what he has done (Prov. 19:17).

If you are looking for a place to invest your money, what safer place, or what greater return, than to invest in the poor? Your investment will not be insured by the U.S. government, but by the Lord God Himself. He is surety for the poor. But there are a few restrictions He imposes before He accepts your deposit in His CD (Certificate of Devotion). First, you need genuine pity and compassion for the poor and dispossessed. Second, understand that the CD will not be liquid; you may not get your principal and interest back in this life. But you will get it back, and with great reward (Matt. 6:19-21).

Jesus prophesied that we would always have the poor with us (Matt. 26:11). The reasons for this are complex, of course. But one thing is sure: as long as the poor are with us, we are to declare our own personal war on poverty, not relying on humanistic governments, but revealing what is in our own hearts. Then, when we meet Christ on that day, He will say to us, "Come, you who are blessed of my Father, take your inheritance . . . For I was hungry and you gave me something to eat, I was thirsty and you gave me something to drink" (Matt. 25:34-35).

Scriptural Examples

The Samaritan. Jesus told of a man who took pity on one who lay beaten and bleeding on the side of the road. The Samaritan bandaged the man's wounds, put him on his own donkey, then took him to an inn and paid the innkeeper to look after him. Jesus says, "Go and do likewise" (Luke 10:33-37).

The deacons. In the early Church, a dispute arose about the distribution of food to the poor. The disciples met together and selected seven men to serve as deacons. The deacons were to ensure that the poor were properly cared for (Acts 6:1-5).

Prayer of Application

Father, give me a real heart for the poor and needy, for those who are homeless, and for those who languish in prisons. They need both humankindness and Your words of mercy and hope.

Treat Everyone with Dignity and Kindness

He who despises his neighbor sins, but blessed is he who is kind to the needy (Prov. 14:21).

Dr. R. C. Sproul asks this: "What is the one question to which everyone will answer 'Yes?'" The question is, "Do you want to be treated with dignity?" Every person is created in the image of God (Gen. 1:27). While sin has defaced that image, people deserve proper respect because of it (1 Pet. 2:17). Christ came to seek and to save the lost, such as these (Luke 19:10).

We are often tempted to despise our neighbor who is poor or different (Prov. 14:20). But we must not forget that the gap between the poor and us is infinitely more narrow than is the gap between Christ and us. He made Himself poor, that we might become rich in heavenly things. By being merciful, we remember Christ's sacrifice for us, and so honor Him.

But there's another reason for mercy here. We are promised that our mercy will bring us blessedness. Our Lord even compared acts of kindness toward the poor as commensurate with doing the same thing for Him (Matt. 25:34-40). The blessings of the Lord will abound to him who shares his food with the hungry, and provides the homeless with shelter (Isa. 58:6-8).

Scriptural Examples

The Shunammite woman. Whenever the prophet Elisha would pass by Shunem, this well-to-do woman would fix him a meal. Later, she and her husband prepared a room in which he would stay. The prophet would bless her in turn (2 Kings 4:8-24).

Job. Job said that it was his business to be kind to the poor, to be a father to the needy, eyes for the blind, and feet for the lame. Job took up the cause of the stranger (Job 29:11-16).

The church at Antioch. Following a prophecy by Agabus, these people collected a generous offering for the saints in Judea, and sent it via Barnabas and Paul (Acts 11:28-30).

Prayer of Application

Lord, help me to treat everyone with dignity, especially those who are poor in this world, serving them physically and telling them of the One who came to enrich them eternally.

In Wisdom, Find Compassion for Others

*Do not withhold good from those who deserve it, when it is in
your power to act. Do not say to your neighbor, "Come back later;
I'll give it tomorrow"—when you now have it with you*
(Prov. 3:27-28).

Not only are we obligated to seek kindness and mercy for our
neighbor, but we are to seek it in a timely manner. The person who
says, "Come back tomorrow," is devious in hoping that the needs
of her neighbor will somehow disappear, be forgotten, or that her
neighbor will find help elsewhere.

The very underpinning of wisdom and of God's law is that we
love God and love our neighbor as ourselves (Lev. 19:18; Matt.
5:43-45; 22:38-39; Luke 10:27; Gal. 5:14). This foundational
commandment leaves no room for selfishness or procrastination.
We are to seek the highest good for our neighbor, not as a
secondary motive behind that of serving self, but as primary, and
thus influencing all of our actions on the earth.

The wisdom that is of the world says, "Look out for number
one"—yourself. Selfishness is the root of pride, which is the root
of sin, which is the root of all of the problems the world faces. Only
in the self*less*ness of living to meet the needs of others can we find
the peace, joy, and fulfillment that Christ brings.

Scriptural Examples

The old man in Gibeah. This old man came in tired from a
long day's work and met a traveler in the city square. He knew there
were wicked men in his city just as there were in Sodom in the days
of Lot. In kindness and true hospitality, the old man took the
traveler home and fed both him and his donkeys (Judg. 19:16-21).

Boaz. The law required that field owners allow the poor and
alien to glean the leftovers of the crop (Lev. 19:9-10). Ruth, who
was both poor and an alien in Israel, came to glean in the field of
Boaz. He went beyond what the law required (Ruth 2).

Prayer of Application

Father, help me to gain more compassion for my neighbors
and to look for ways to be of service to them, particularly those who
are my brothers and sisters in the household of faith.

Humbly Come to the Aid of the Needy

The Lord tears down the proud man's house but he keeps the widow's boundaries intact (**Prov. 15:25**).

God reigns supreme over this world, a fact suppressed by the natural woman (Rom. 1:18-21), who does as she pleases without regard to eternal consequences. But the woman who lifts herself up in pride and treason against her Creator will destroy not only herself, but her whole house as well. Pride is in many ways the chief of sins because it elevates self over others.

God upholds the cause of the widow, the orphan, and all who are downtrodden. The early church established the office of deacon specifically to care for those in need (Acts 6:1-3). We, too, are enjoined to take up the widow's cause (James 1:27). God is their Friend and Benefactor. He establishes their boundaries.

But proud scoffers beware! Do not be deceived. If you fail to honor God with your riches and share your blessings with those in need, know this: God does not settle all of His accounts in this life. Read Jesus' story about Lazarus and the rich man (in Luke 16:20 and following), and tremble.

Scriptural Examples

Naomi and Ruth. God provided for these widows. Naomi was blessed by her faithful daughter-in-law. God blessed Ruth through Boaz, her kinsman-redeemer (the book of Ruth).

The prophet's widow. This woman cried out to Elisha as her dead husband's creditor came to enslave her two sons. Elisha told her to gather up jars, into which God poured oil. She sold the oil to pay the debt she owed (2 Kings 4:1-7).

The Shunammite woman. Elisha restored her son's life and then told her to avoid the coming famine by going to Philistia. Seven years later, she returned to Israel at precisely the time that the king was being told of Elisha's miracle. The king gave her back her land, and seven years' income from it (2 Kings 8:1-6).

Prayer of Application

Father, in the riches of Your grace You take up the cause of the poor and powerless. Give me a real heart for the needy so I may become a representative of Your love for them.

See God's Providence in the Trials of Others

He who mocks the poor shows contempt for their Maker; whoever gloats over disaster will not go unpunished (Prov. 17:5).

In an attempt to elevate their status, some men and women mock those they consider less than themselves. Bob remembers growing up in Tennessee when African-Americans were looked upon as almost sub-human by many whites, including some who professed to be Christians. Racial discrimination still goes on, and it is a reproach and sin against our Maker.

The spiritual woman should see God in control of every circumstance. Where there are poor people, it is not necessarily due to their bad fortune or laziness, so much as it is to the providence of the God who made them (1 Sam. 2:7; Prov. 22:2). She who laughs at the condition of the poor utters treason against God (Prov. 17:5). This is particularly true when disaster falls upon others.

Rather, the Bible teaches that we are to sympathize with the victims of calamities, lifting them up in prayer and providing for them in acts of lovingkindness (Prov. 24:17; 25:21; Rom. 12:20). The Bible teaches that every person is made in the image of his Creator (Gen. 1:26). Although fallen, each individual on this planet should be treated with dignity and respect.

Scriptural Examples

Moses. He led the Israelites, who sang of the defeat of Pharaoh. They were not gloating, but bringing honor and glory to the Lord God who had done it (Ex. 15).

Shimei. As David fled from Absalom's conspiracy, this Benjamite cursed him and pelted him with stones. David held his peace, for he said that the Lord may be instructing Shimei to curse him. Or maybe the Lord would see David's distress and repay him with good for the curses of Shemei (2 Sam. 16:5-13).

Job. Even in his distress Job said he never sinned against God by rejoicing at his enemy's misfortune (Job 31:28-30).

Prayer of Application

Sovereign Lord, You have made all things for Your glory and eternal purpose, including the poor, and even the evil man for the day of destruction. Help me to respect every person.

Treat Animals with Kindness

*A righteous man cares for the needs of his animal, but the kindest
acts of the wicked are cruel* (Prov. 12:10).

The animal kingdom has suffered greatly under fallen mankind. They have been under a curse because of man's sin (Gen. 6:
7,17). Even today, the whole creation groans under the burden of
man's rebellion against God (Rom. 8:22).

We should not add to this suffering by being cruel to beasts, be
they livestock or pets. An animal cannot testify to our cruelty, so
the wicked person thinks he or she can get away with it. Even our
tender mercies can be cruel. A person tightly chains a dog to keep
it out of the street and performs a cruelty to the dog that may be
worse than death under the wheels of a speeding car. Perhaps she
beats her dog, thinking it will benefit the dog as it learns to obey.
All the while, the dog has no understanding as to why it is being
struck, and the beating is in vain.

Beware, wicked people! Every animal belongs to the Lord (Ps.
50:10-12). He knows every bird and fish and creeping thing (Matt.
6:26). Those we kill for food should be dispatched painlessly. God
expects us to treat all animals with kindness.

Scriptural Examples

Jacob. On their return to meet Esau, Jacob's family drove large
herds that included ewes and cows with young. He moved slowly
on his journey, and upon arrival, built shelters for all of his
livestock. He explained to his brother that if he drove his animals
too fast, they would die (Gen. 33:13, 17).

Balaam. His donkey veered off the road into a field when it saw
the angel of the Lord standing there, holding a drawn sword. Balaam
beat his beast to get it back on the road. The donkey pressed against
a wall, so he beat her again. Finally, the animal lay down under
Balaam. The wicked Balaam beat the donkey again until the animal
spoke and the angel appeared to him, too (Num. 22:22-31).

Prayer of Application

Dear God, thank You for the pets that we own and also the
animals which provide the meat that we eat. Help us never to
subject animals to pain or torment, but to respect Your creation.

Study Questions and Projects

1) What promise is the merciful person given in Psalm 18:25? In Psalm 37:25-26? In Proverbs 3:3-4? In Proverbs 21:21? In Matthew 5:7?

2) With what other important elements of the Christian life is mercy (love) linked in Hosea 4:1? Why do you suppose this is so? Discuss with others. (Compare the verse in Hosea with Matthew 23:23.)

3) What are some of the qualities of mercy that Paul speaks of in Colossians 3:12-13?

a) _____

b) _____

c) _____

d) _____

e) _____

f) _____

g) _____

4). Read 2 Timothy 1:16-18. What did Onesiphorus do for Paul? What was Paul's prayer for him? Do you have a "Paul" in your life whom you could help?

Other Verses to Study

Leviticus 19:34; Zechariah 7:9-10; Ephesians 4:32; 1 Peter 3:8; 1 John 3:17-18.

One to Memorize

He who is kind to the poor lends to the Lord, and he will reward him for what he has done (Prov. 19:17).

My Personal Action Plan to Be a Woman of Mercy

1) _____ 2) _____

3) _____ 4) _____

- Proverbs 31:21-
When it snows, she has no fear for her household;
for all of them are clothed in scarlet.

Chapter Thirteen

A Woman of Christ
•••••••••••••••••••••••••••••

The imagery in this verse can point us to Christ, even though He is not mentioned directly. The whiteness of snow reminds us of Christ's righteousness which is imputed to the believer. As Matthew recounts for us the Transfiguration of our Lord, he says "His appearance was like lightning, and his clothes were white as snow" (Matt. 28:3). Revelation 1:14 says of Christ, "His head and hair were white like wool, as white as snow, and his eyes were like blazing fire."

The clothing of scarlet recalls Christ's blood which is a covering for our sins. As Paul says in Ephesians 1:7, "In him we have redemption through his blood, the forgiveness of sins, in accordance with the riches of God's grace." Hebrews 9:22 picks up on that same theme, saying, "In fact, the law requires that nearly everything be cleansed with blood, and without the shedding of blood there is no forgiveness."

But perhaps the greatest verse regarding these two colors is in Isaiah 1:18. "'Come now, let us reason together,' says the Lord. 'Though your sins are like scarlet, they shall be as white as snow; though they are red as crimson, they shall be like wool.'" Praise be to God who imputes our sins to Christ, and who imputes His righteousness to us.

Let Christ Illumine Your Path

The path of the righteous is like the first gleam of dawn, shining ever brighter till the full light of day. But the way of the wicked is like deep darkness; they do not know what makes them stumble (**Prov. 4:18-19**).

Notice here that the path of the righteous begins with the first glimmer of dawn. It begins with a small ray of light and progresses to the fullness of noonday. Christ is that "dawn's early light," as He is our "bright Morning Star" (Rev. 22:16).

In Matthew 7:13-14, Jesus speaks of the "narrow and wide gates," the former leading to life, and the latter to destruction. Let's look at these proverbs closely and see if they can help us define the narrow versus the wide gates.

Imagine a funnel that is narrow at one end and wide at the other. Entering at the wide end, the way gets narrower and narrower, darker and darker, until it finally ends in destruction. This is the way of the sinner who does not repent. It is also the way of the legalist who thinks she can justify herself by good works.

Now turn the funnel around and enter at the narrow end. It is narrow because one can only enter it by the gate marked "The Lord Jesus Christ" (John 14:6; Acts 4:12; John 10:9). He is our light (John 8:12), and as we walk with Him down His path, the funnel gets wider and wider as we discover the truth of God.

Scriptural Examples

The Pharisees. These men represented themselves as lights of Israel, but in reality they were "blind guides." They were legalists, men who placed extra-biblical requirements upon those who followed their ways. They entered at the "wide" gate and stumbled in the darkness (Matt. 23).

Satan. Satan is also known as Lucifer, which means "angel of light." He poses as an angel of light (2 Cor. 11:14), but is in fact the author of darkness and blindness (2 Cor. 4:4).

Prayer of Application

Heavenly Father, thank You for opening the door to salvation in the person of the Lord Jesus Christ. As I grow in Christ, how warm the light of His brightness is to me.

Hide in Christ, Your Ransom

The wicked become a ransom for the righteous, and the unfaithful for the upright (**Prov. 21:18**).

What irony! Jesus, the Righteous One, gave His life as a ransom for many (Matt. 20:28)—the Upright for the unfaithful. How then can the unfaithful become a ransom for the upright?

As a God of absolute righteousness and justice, God cannot overlook sin, and demands that a ransom, or payment, be made. Interestingly, there are instances in redemptive history where the wicked have become such a "ransom" for others.

When Moses went up on the mountain to meet God, the people talked Aaron into fashioning a gold idol. When Moses came back, he told the Levites to go through the camp with their swords and kill their brothers, friends, and neighbors. About 3,000 people died. Later, God also struck the people with a plague for their sin. But Aaron did not die by the sword or in the plague. God's anger against this "righteous" man was assuaged in the ransom paid by those who did die (Exod. 32:1–33:6).

Paul tells us that the righteous Jesus became a curse for us that we might be redeemed (Gal. 3:13). He who knew no sin became sin, so that we might become the righteousness of God in Him (2 Cor. 5:21). Those who are hidden in Him, and in His ransom, will avoid the punishment reserved for the wicked.

Scriptural Examples

Aachan. He withheld some of the plunder of Jericho. The Israelites stoned Aachan and his family to death. They were a ransom assuaging the fierce anger of God (Josh. 7:24-26).

Egypt and Ethiopia. They were ransom for Jerusalem as God turned Sennacherib from the city (Isa. 43:3-4; 2 Kings 19:7-9).

The firstborn of Egypt. These people, many perhaps mere babies, were used as a ransom for the deliverance of God's people from Egypt (Hos. 11:1; Ex. 11:4-8; 12:29-36).

Prayer of Application

Dear Lord, thank You for sending Jesus to the cross to pay the ransom for the sins of all who would be saved. I thank You, Lord, that it was effective and actually secured my salvation.

Be Bold in the Righteousness of Christ

The wicked man ("lawless," KJV) flees though no one pursues, but the righteous are as bold as a lion (Prov. 28:1).

We love Psalm 23, and particularly the verse that says, "Surely goodness and love will follow me all the days of my life." The woman of God who, like David, has been made righteous by the righteousness imputed to her by Christ, confidently expects the goodness and grace of her Lord to follow her everywhere she goes (Rom. 8:28). The natural woman should expect exactly the opposite. She should look nervously over her shoulder, anticipating only wrath and anger (Rom. 2:8).

We're told by modern psychologists that mankind's problems stem from a guilt complex. If people could only get rid of their guilt, they would be able to toss off their fears and anxieties, their phobias and their psychoses. But the Bible says that our guilt can only be washed away by the blood of Christ. Guilt is real, and its cause is self-seeking sin and the rejection of the truth of God.

Throughout Scripture, the Messiah is known as the Lion of Judah (Gen. 49:9 ; Hos. 5:14 ; 11:10; Rev. 5:5). Christ is that Lion, and His righteous ones may be as bold as He is. No longer beset with guilt that causes us to fear, the Christian can look forward with confidence (Phil. 3:13). Her Master and Brother is not just king of the jungle, but King of kings!

Scriptural Examples

Adam and Eve. Following their sin they hid in the garden. Why? Because they were afraid. Although they were naked before the Fall, it was the shame and guilt of their sin that exposed their nakedness to their eyes, and brought fear (Gen. 3:9-10).

Caleb and Joshua. While the other ten spies at Kadesh Barnea were fearful of giants, these men were as bold as lions, and confidently argued for an immediate attack and occupation of the land that God had promised to them (Num. 14:6-10).

Prayer of Application

Sovereign Lord, You are truly the Lion of Judah. Even today You are in control of all things. Make me bold, Lord, in the knowledge that through Your strengthening, I can do all things.

Be a Soul Winner

The fruit of the righteous is a tree of life, and he who
wins souls is wise (Prov. 11:30).

The Tree of Life is seen in the Garden of Eden (Gen. 2:9; 3:22-24) and in the book of Revelation (2:7; 22:2, 14, 19). It holds out the promise of eternal life to whomever eats of its fruit. (The phrase "tree of life" also appears in Proverbs 3:18; 13:12; and 15:4.) Following their eviction, Adam and Eve saw cherubim with flaming swords guarding the gates to the garden's Tree of Life.

In Revelation quite a different picture is given. Those whose robes are washed are allowed to eat of the fruit of the Tree. Oh, the marvelous grace of our God, who turns our sin, rebellion, and consequent death into the joy of eternal life with Him!

As bondslaves of Christ, we are called to bear the fruit of righteousness that only comes through Him (Phil. 1:11; Gal. 5:22-25). We are, as it were, trees of life planted in this world, and as Christ's ministers of reconciliation (2 Cor. 5:18) we are to show forth the fruit of eternal life to all people everywhere.

Scriptural Examples

Jonah. Jonah was called by God to go to Nineveh and to be a "tree of life." Instead, he rebelled and ran the other way. We're afraid we are often like Jonah, refusing to hold out the Tree of Life to a world that is swallowed by sin (Jonah 1:1–3:10).

The apostles. When told not preach the gospel, Peter exclaimed that they "must obey God rather than men." With joy they held forth the Tree of Life (Acts 5:16-29; 40-42).

Paul. Paul won many souls for the Lord. He hoped that his ministry to the Gentiles might cause his own countrymen to respond in repentance and faith (Rom. 11:13-14).

The righteous wife. Peter advised wives how to win their husbands to the Lord: through the purity and reverence of their lives, as they exhibited the fruits of the Spirit (1 Pet. 3:1-2).

Prayer of Application

Father, thank You for Your gospel of grace. Not through any works of mine am I saved, but only through the life and death of Christ, my Savior. Help me to share this Tree of Life with others.

Beware of the Ultimate Lie

A corrupt witness mocks at justice, and the mouth of the wicked gulps down evil. Penalties are prepared for mockers, and beatings for the backs of fools (**Prov. 19:28-29**).

Even if the Bible didn't teach it, "justice" makes sense as an eternal concept. Adolf Hitler mocked justice when he committed suicide in his Berlin bunker. But he only fled the hands of angry men to drop into the hands of an angry God.

In these verses we see the person who mocks justice by lying and who gulps down evil with her mouth. All the while this person sets a trap for herself. In the end, her contempt for justice will form the basis of her judgment. She scorns the free gift of salvation that God offers (Eph. 2:8-9).

Have you ever wondered what would be the biggest lie one could tell—one that's a 15 on a scale of 1 to 10? John says that the person who claims to be a Christian but who does not do what Christ commands "is a liar and the truth is not in him" (1 John 2:4). We believe that to mock Christ's atoning work, all the while posturing as His follower, is the ultimate lie. Peter says it would have been better not to have known the way of salvation than to turn one's back on the Savior (2 Pet. 2:21). Beware of mocking the ultimate Judge (Acts 17:31).

Scriptural Examples

Joseph's brothers. They lied to their father, giving him false evidence that Joseph was dead. They mocked judgment, but received mercy at the hands of their brother, and were spared—like us—the punishment they so richly deserved (Gen. 37:31-35).

The Pharisees and teachers of the Law. While posing as men of God, these men told the ultimate lie. They practiced "godliness" with their lips, but their hearts were far from God (Matt. 15:7-9). Jesus mocked these mockers, these "blind guides" who nibbled at righteousness but gulped down evil (Matt. 23).

Prayer of Application

Heavenly Father, may I never betray You by paying You lip service while living a life that belies what I say. I can only do this through the power of Your Spirit sustaining me.

Warn Yourself and Others of Self-Delusion

*There is a way that seems right to a man, but in the end
it leads to death* (**Prov. 16:25**).

Since Adam's fall, mankind's heart has been radically affected.
Although a person thinks she knows what is good for her, the Bible
says that she is blind (John 12:40; 2 Cor. 4:4) and cannot know the
truth. Jesus described the Pharisees as "blind guides," who taught
self-salvation—a false teaching that did not come from God.

Today, many in the visible church are being led by modern
"blind guides." They are deluded into thinking that the way to
reconciliation with God is through their good works, or taking
some external sacrament. Others teach that it's not important what
a person believes about God, so long as her belief is sincere. There
are many such ways that lead to death, but Jesus says that He is the
only way to life (John 14:6). A person must be regenerated, or born
from above (John 3:3). Only then is blindness healed and spiritual
truth clearly and savingly discerned (Acts 9:18).

Every man-made religion in the world is what may be termed
"auto-soteric." That is, if you want to reach heaven, you must do
it yourself. This seems so right to fallen man, but in the end it leads
to death. *Only* biblical Christianity is different. It is "hetero-
soteric." The saving is done by God through Christ's atoning work
alone. Ours is an external righteousness. It is not of ourselves.

Scriptural Examples

Lot. Lot and Abram's herdsmen argued over grazing land, and
the two agreed to part company. Lot decided to settle in the land
that looked best, down by Sodom. There was a way that seemed
right to Lot, but in the end it brought trouble (Gen. 13:7-12).

Saul. In opposition to the word of the Lord, Saul did what he
thought best and did not kill all of the captured sheep and cattle.
Samuel rebuked him for going his own way. Ultimately he was
stripped of his kingdom (1 Sam. 15:20-22).

Prayer of Application

Dear Father, thank You for sending Your only Son as a sacrifice
for my sins. He is the only way to reconciliation with You. Help
me to be a true witness of His gospel of grace.

Study Questions and Projects

1) The Bible is full of examples of "types" of the Savior, such as the colors white and scarlet. They are sometimes called the "shadow" while Christ is the "reality" (Col. 2:17). Read the following verses and write down the types or shadows you find, then the office or aspect of Christ to which they point.

a) Exodus 12:21 with 1 Corinthians 5:7: _____

_____

b) Exodus 27:1-2 with Hebrews 13:10: _____

_____

c) Exodus 30:18-20 with Ephesians 5:26-27: _____

_____

d) Exodus 40:21 with Hebrews 10:20: _____

_____

e) Exodus 16:31 with John 6:32-35: _____

_____

f) Numbers 21:9 with John 3:14-15: _____

_____

2) How does Jesus say in John 14:15 that we will be able to know that we truly love Him? How are others to recognize that we are His disciples? (John 13:35)

Other Verses to Study
Leviticus 11:44; Luke 11:27-28; 1 John 2:3-6; 5:3.

One to Memorize
The fruit of the righteous is a tree of life, and he who wins souls is wise (Prov. 11:30).

My Personal Action Plan to Be a Woman of Christ

1)_____ 2)_____

3)_____ 4)_____

- **Proverbs 31:22** -
She makes coverings for her bed;
she is clothed in fine linen and purple.

Chapter Fourteen

A Woman of Godliness
•••••••••••••••••••••••••••••••

In Proverbs 31:22 we see the virtuous woman "clothed in fine linen and purple." Fine linen and purple were the apparel of the wealthy (Luke 16:19), and were used extensively in the tabernacle in the wilderness (Exod. 35). There, purple and fine linen spoke of royal glory and practical righteousness. This godly woman of Proverbs is wearing clothes that clearly indicate her holy character and dignity (Ironside, *Proverbs-Song of Solomon*, p. 479).

The goal of the Christian life is to be conformed to the image of Christ (Rom. 8:29). Paul exhorts us in Romans 12:1-2: "Therefore, I urge you…in view of God's mercy, to offer your bodies as living sacrifices, holy and pleasing to God—this is your spiritual act of worship. Do not conform any longer to the pattern of this world, but be transformed by the renewing of your mind. Then you will be able to test and approve what God's will is—His good, pleasing and perfect will." We are to be transformed in holiness and godliness by the renewing of our minds.

How are we transformed into Christ's likeness? By feeding on His Word, and by obedience to it. In other words, what you are doing right now. As Paul told Timothy, "For physical training is of some value, but godliness has value for all things, holding promise for both the present life and the life to come" (1 Tim. 4:8).

Know the Way of Holiness

I, wisdom, dwell together with prudence; I possess knowledge and discretion. To fear the Lord is to hate evil; I hate pride and arrogance, evil behavior and perverse speech (**Prov.** 8:12-13).

In these verses, wisdom speaks in the first person; wisdom is personified. In verses 1-11 of this chapter, we see wisdom as the Word of God in its spoken form. Here (John 1:1-14) we find it in its embodied form: the person of our Lord Jesus Christ.

Jesus said that throughout history many would come in His name, saying "I am Christ," and would deceive many (Matt. 24:5; Mark 13:6; Luke 21:8). In fact, many different Christs are being preached throughout the world today (1 John 4:1-3). For instance, many teach that He was a great teacher, but not God incarnate. But the true Christ, the Christ of Scripture, is distinguished by His call to holiness. This call is seen here, and it takes two forms.

First, there is a call to understand *who* He is. He is the Majestic God, Creator (John 1:1), and Sustainer (Heb. 1:3) of all that is visible and invisible. He alone is worthy of our worship. He is altogether righteous and holy, set apart, transcendent in utter wisdom, knowledge, perfection, and power. He will one day destroy evil by the power of His coming (Mal. 3:2; 2 Thess. 2:8).

The second call is to understand who *we* are. We are prideful, arrogant, and prone to evil behavior and perverse speech. The way of holiness leads only by the cross of Christ, where the holiness of God met the sinfulness of mankind.

Scriptural Examples

Isaiah. God's prophet saw a vision of the Lord in his temple. Angelic beings sang out, "Holy, holy, holy is the Lord Almighty." In contrast, Isaiah saw himself as a man of unclean lips, of perverse and evil speech, living among a people of uncleanliness and perversity. But, by His grace, God seared Isaiah's lips and took away his sin and guilt (Isa. 6:1-8; Eph. 2:8-9).

Prayer of Application

Heavenly Father, thank You for the sacrifice of Your Son, who provided the payment for the crime and debt of sin, and imputed the righteousness of His sinless life to people like me.

Be a Peacemaker

A hot-tempered man stirs up dissension, but a patient man calms a quarrel (**Prov. 15:18**).

Our very salvation comes as a result of God's slowness to anger (2 Peter 3:15). Patience and self-control are fruits of the Spirit of God (Gal. 5:22). So we who bear that Spirit in our hearts are called by Christ to be peacemakers (Matt. 5:9).

When we or someone we love are treated unjustly, we often think that we need to give full vent to our feelings and stand up for our rights. While we may need to express our concerns, God requires that we live godly lives in witness of the One who brings peace. Anger and wrath do not bring about the righteousness of God (James 1:20). We are challenged to live supernaturally. We are called to reflect a higher wisdom than that of the natural woman. We are called to lives of patience.

But how do we put this principle in shoe leather? First, we need to rely fully upon the work of the Holy Spirit in our lives to control our tempers and our anger. Second, we need to realize that God is sovereign over all things, and that we can submit to the circumstances of our lives knowing that He will never leave us nor forsake us. Finally, we need to have firmly planted in our minds and hearts that a hot temper is a reflection of our depravity. As sin, it does not bring unity, but separation.

Scriptural Examples

Abraham. When his herdsmen and those of Lot began to quarrel over pastures, Abraham suggested that they part company so that there would be pastureland for all (Gen. 13:7-9).

Isaac. Gerar's servants quarrelled with Isaac over the ownership of a well. Isaac moved his flocks to another well, and then to another, until peace was restored (Gen. 26:19-22).

Jephthah. He was driven from his home by his half brothers. Desiring peace, he settled in the land of Tob (Judg. 11:1-3).

Prayer of Application

Lord, You have called us to be reflections of You, and as such to be peacemakers. Help me to do this by acknowledging You as sovereign Lord and trusting only You for justice.

Be Patient, for Your God Is Sovereign

A patient man has great understanding, but a quick-tempered man displays folly (Prov. 14:29).

The natural person who is patient may fear reprisal or just be apathetic. But the Christian has a deep principle from which to draw. Her God is sovereign over His creation and is working all things out for His own glory, and for the ultimate good of those He has called (Rom. 8:28-29). Therefore, the Christian doesn't need to "stuff" her feelings, which only leads to more anger later. Conversely, the above principle, if allowed to take root in one's heart, dissipates anger and allows the love of Christ to shine through the Christian in the most difficult circumstances.

We are not to repay evil for evil, but to try to live at peace with everyone, leaving revenge to God alone. We are to treat our enemies with kindness, repaying evil with good. Then we may "heap burning coals upon his head" (Rom. 12:17-21), coals which may bring repentance as he or she sees our understanding.

This is not to say that there is not a time for righteous anger. But there is a vast difference between a temper tantrum and godly anger which does not sin (Eph. 4:26). Godly anger seeks to control passion with reason. It doesn't seek anyone's harm, but rather the correction of injustice in a godly manner.

Scriptural Examples

Asa. He was enraged by Hanani's reproof and threw him into prison. Soon after, Asa was stricken with a disease. Because he failed to seek God's healing, he died of it (2 Chron. 16:7-14).

Jesus. Our Lord had both the right and the power to save Himself and avoid the cross, but He patiently endured all these things to bring salvation to His people (Heb. 5:7-10).

The prophets. These men were examples of patience in the face of injustice, suffering, and oppression. Their understanding of the One they represented made the difference (James 5:10).

Prayer of Application

Father, how easily I get angry when I sense injustice. Help me to patiently understand that You are in control of all things, and that You are working every event toward Your glory.

Bear Fruit that Comes from Christ Alone

The wicked desire the plunder of evil men, but the root of the righteous flourishes (Prov. 12:12).

This proverb sets forth the differences in thinking between the wicked and the righteous. The wicked person believes that she will find success in the ways of other evil people. A few years ago, the savings and loan crisis was in the headlines. With it came the prosecution of people who had imitated one another in deceiving others. They devised a *net* (KJV) for the unwary, and figured that they would get rich from the *plunder*. The wicked emulate the cunning plans of others, and those plans lead to destruction.

The righteous person thinks in terms of a vine, or tree. The *root* and trunk of the tree is Christ, and each believer is a branch (John 15:5). Branches *bear* fruit, but roots *produce* fruit. Unattached to the root system the branch will wither and die. It has no life in itself, but must look for its success in the life-support system of its attachment to the root. It is imperative for the Christian to recognize his or her powerlessness apart from the sustaining power of Christ. Godliness does not exist apart from Christ.

Scriptural Examples

Haman. This wicked man sought for a net with which to destroy Mordecai and the Jews (Est. 3:6). He built a gallows, but he himself was hanged upon it (Est. 7:10).

David. David spoke of the cunning plans of evil men who sought his life. He described their plots against him as a net that had been hidden in a pit they had dug in the ground. He asked the Lord (his root) for their downfall. David's enemies were trapped in the same net they laid for him (Ps. 35:7-8; 57:6).

Daniel. Daniel was rooted in the love of God. As a branch, he resolved in his heart that he would bring forth fruit unto God, and he did so abundantly (Dan. 1:8).

Prayer of Application

Dear Lord, thank You for grafting me into the Tree of Life. By myself I am lost and can do nothing of eternal significance. But because I am attached to the Vine, I can do all things through Him.

Let Purity Dominate Your Thought Life

Death and Destruction lie open before the Lord—how much more the hearts of men (**Prov. 15:11**).

There is no place in all of creation that is not open and visible to our omniscient, omnipresent God. He sees into the hearts and minds of every man and woman. The natural person scoffs at such a notion and goes on thinking sinful thoughts.

In contrast, the child of God understands that God has access to her thoughts. She allows God to direct her thoughts (Gal. 5:16-18), for she knows that thoughts always precede actions. The impurities that remain in her mind remind her of her sinfulness and urge her toward a closer walk with Christ.

How do you allow God to direct your thoughts? One way may be to think of your mind as a blackboard. Ask God to write on it only thoughts that are pleasing to Him. What thoughts are pleasing to God? Whatever is true, noble, right, pure, lovely, admirable, excellent, or praiseworthy, think about such things, "and the God of peace will be with you" (Phil. 4:8-9).

Scriptural Examples

Aaron. His rebellious thoughts were known to God as surely as were Moses' angry words and swift rod at the waters of Meribah (Num. 20:12, 24).

Nebuchadnezzar. This Babylonian king wanted his wise men not only to interpret his dream, but to tell him exactly what the dream was. God gave Daniel the dream that the king would not tell anyone, thereby allowing Daniel to witness to the omniscience of Almighty God (Dan. 2:29ff).

The Jews. Jehovah said that He would punish the Hebrews who merely *thought* that He would not act (Zeph. 1:12).

The Pharisees. Jesus knew the evil thoughts these adversaries harbored in their minds. He read their minds like a book, and often answered them before they spoke (Luke 5:22).

Prayer of Application

Dear Lord, purify my thoughts. May every one of them come into subjection to Your will. Search my mind, O Lord, see if there are any wicked thoughts there and purify it.

Hunger for Righteousness

*He who is full loathes honey, but to the hungry even what is
bitter tastes sweet* (**Prov. 27:7**).

Think back to that last Thanksgiving dinner when you ate too
much turkey and mashed potatoes and gravy. One more piece of
pumpkin pie sure looked good, but you knew that it would only
add to your misery. You wished you were hungry again, didn't you?

Most Americans have been gorged with belongings and food.
We seek larger homes and fancier cars. We long for more exotic
foods and wilder entertainment to satisfy our jaded tastes. In
contrast, all along the Mexican border many illegal immigrants
cross the border at night, hungrily seeking the jobs that would be
beneath most of us. What is *bitter* to us is *sweet* to them.

For the woman whose spiritual eyes have been opened, a
hunger begins for the things of God—His Word and His righteousness. Then, after time, sometimes this hunger has a way of
abating. The person may feel full and no longer in need of the pure
food of the Word (Heb. 5:13). She grows spiritually slothful and
fat, satisfied with far less than God has for her. Have you been
"spiritually stuffed"? We know *we* have.

But Jesus says, "Blessed are they who hunger and thirst after
righteousness, for they shall be filled" (Matt. 5:6). We need the
Word to convict us of sin, and to convince us of our need for its
healing and sustaining power. Perhaps we should not pray for
more food. Perhaps we should pray for more hunger.

Scriptural Examples

The sinful woman. Jesus welcomed the hunger of this woman.
While she washed His feet and anointed them with perfume, His
hosts complained of her presence (Luke 7:47).

The Laodiceans. These self-satisfied churchgoers thought
they had it made. But Jesus rebuked them, saying, "You are
wretched, pitiful, poor, blind and naked" (Rev. 3:17).

Prayer of Application

Father, thank You for the Word which helps me to grow in
righteousness as I am guided by Your Spirit. I confess that
sometimes I feel stuffed and unwilling to eat. Make me hungry.

Study Questions and Projects

1) Read 1 Corinthians 3:16-17. To what building does Paul compare the believer? Why? Is it important to keep the building holy? Why?

2) Read 2 Corinthians 10:3-5. Discuss these verses with others. What kind of warfare is Paul speaking of here? What kind of power is available to us? According to verse 5, how many of our thoughts are to be obedient to Christ?

3) On what basis are we to be married to Christ, according to 2 Corinthians 11:3? Why is that important to God? How does Paul say we can be led astray in verse 4? What spiritually adulterous problem did some of the Corinthians have to which Paul alludes in verse 5?

4) What does Paul say teams up with godliness to be of great gain or value to us? (1 Tim. 6:6)

5) In 2 Peter 1:5-7, the apostle gives us a list of things we are to add to our faith. They are: _____, _____,

_____, _____, _____,

_____, _____. What reason does he give for this in verse 8? In verse 9, he says that those who do not have them are _____ and _____.

Other Verses to Study
Leviticus 11:44-45; Psalm 24:3-5; 119:1-3; Ephesians 4:20-24.

One to Memorize
A patient man has great understanding, but a quick-tempered man displays folly (Prov. 14:29).

My Personal Action Plan to Be a Woman of Godliness

1) _____ 2) _____

3) _____ 4) _____

- Proverbs 31:23 -
Her husband is respected at the city gate,
where he takes his seat among the elders of the land.

Chapter Fifteen

A Woman of Submission

Amy's mother tells the story of when Amy was a young child and was repeatedly told to "sit down" at the dinner table. Finally, Amy sat down but said in a defiant voice, "I may be sitting down, but inside I'm standing up!"

This story tells us that submission goes much deeper than we often realize. Because of sin working in us, we rebel against God, our parents, and others in authority. This is clearly seen in the marriage relationship. Christians are called to submit to Christ, and to each other out of reverence for Christ. Wives are to submit to their husbands, and husbands are to love their wives (Eph. 5:21-25). The wisdom woman's husband is respected by the elders at the gate of the city, even as she also respects him (Eph. 5:33).

Some have seen the Bible's teaching of wifely submission as God's punishment upon women. Nothing could be further from the truth! God's precepts are ultimately for our *freedom*. Consider Jepthah, whose mother was a prostitute (Judg. 11). Illegitimate children weren't even allowed to go to church, much less hold an office (Deut. 23:2). Yet Jepthah is honored in God's "Hall of Fame" (Heb. 11:34). Jepthah's "restriction" was not ultimately punitive, but helped to define his calling. So it is with all who honor God by submitting to His established authority—God honors them.

If You Love Christ, Submit to Him

He who obeys instructions guards his life, but he who is contemptuous of his ways will die (Prov. 19:16).

Following His resurrection, Jesus asked Simon Peter three times, "Do you love me?" Each time, after Peter answered in the affirmative, Jesus said, "Feed my sheep" (John 21:15-17). Jesus was telling Peter that Peter's faith in Christ was to be put into action. He was calling Peter and the others, as well as you and I, to be doers of the Word, and not hearers only (James 1:22). Putting your faith to work by submitting to Christ is the secret of victorious living.

Without Christ we can do nothing (John 15:5). Whoever lives by the truth comes to the light so it may be seen that her deeds have been done through God (John 3:21). He'll supply the opportunity, the strength and gifts to carry the work out through the power of the Holy Spirit working in us.

But what are Christ's commandments? Look first to Jesus' words in the four Gospels. Then observe the works of the apostles in Acts. Next, look carefully at the apostles' teaching in the letters and books that make up the rest of the New Testament (John 14:26). Finally, compare all of this with the Ten Commandments (Ex. 20; Deut. 5), and the rest of the Old Testament. We think you will find that Christ's commandments don't omit any of the moral code found there, but enhance our understanding of it.

Scriptural Examples

Joshua. God commanded Moses that upon entering the land, everyone living there was to be put to death. Moses passed this task on to Joshua, who carried it out, but not fully. The people later suffered for it (Josh. 10:40; 11:15).

The disciples. Jesus prayed for His disciples (and for the church) prior to His passion. He said that He had revealed the Father to those the Father had given Him, and that they had obeyed the Father's Word (John 17:7).

Prayer of Application

Heavenly Father, I do love Jesus, and I want to serve Him. By Your Word, teach me His commandments, and then empower me by Your Holy Spirit to joyfully obey them.

Wives, Submit to Your Husbands

Better to live on a corner of the roof than share a house with a quarrelsome wife (Prov. 25:24).

The principle here is quoted from Ephesians 5:22. Actually, the word for "submit" does not occur in the Greek text. It is in verse 21: "Submit to one another out of reverence for Christ." The word *upotassomenoi* is a plural passive participle meaning "subject or subordinate yourselves" to one another.

Just as Christ submitted to the Father, so Christ's church is to to submit to Him. Husbands are to love their wives "just as Christ loved the church and gave himself up for her" (Eph. 5:25-26). Our submission to our husbands comes out of a joyful heart that longs to obey Christ. Submission should *never* be understood as something punitive, but as the way Christ has lovingly ordered His people and provided for their needs.

We recognize that it is difficult to be submissive when one's husband is unsaved, or if he sinfully uses your willingness to submit as an invitation to institute some "power play." But being quarrelsome isn't the answer. As Peter tells us, "Instead [your beauty] should be that of...a gentle and quiet spirit, which is of great worth in God's sight" (1 Pet. 3:4).

All Christians, both men and women, are called to be submissive "to one another out of reverence for Christ" (Eph. 5:21). When we are submissive, we reflect the humility of our Lord who was submissive even to death on the cross for our sake.

Scriptural Examples

Jezebel and Ahab. This couple exhibits the antithesis of God's rule for the home. Ahab was a sniveling rodent who submitted only to evil and the rule of his wife over him. Jezebel's name is synonymous with the rebellious and arrogant wife. She nagged her husband to greater acts of evil, and met her just fate in accordance with the Word of the Lord (1 Kings 21:23-25).

Prayer of Application

Lord God, thank You for Your Word, which gives us direction for godly living. It usually goes against what the world teaches, and submission is no exception. Help me to submit to Christ.

Find the Key to Wisdom in Obedience

The mocker seeks wisdom and finds none, but knowledge comes easily to the discerning (Prov. 14:6).

Jesus states in the Sermon on the Mount that everyone who seeks will find (Matt. 7:7). Here we are told that the mocker seeks wisdom and doesn't find it. A contradiction? Not at all. The fault isn't in Jesus' words. The failure is in the heart of the mocker, who doesn't seek wisdom in readiness to obey it.

If the scorner seeks wisdom at all, it is for her own purposes and sinful interests. She reads the Bible to prove her own presuppositions, rather than to seek what God really has to say. She never searches intending to obey the truth even if she finds it. Therefore, God does not reveal the truth to her.

The true seeker of godly wisdom does so with singleness of mind and purpose, that she might be obedient to it. Otherwise, she'll just be puffed up by it. But godly wisdom is meant to be put to work on a daily basis. The woman who searches for this reason is certain to easily find the wisdom she seeks.

Scriptural Examples

Azariah and Johanan. These men wanted wisdom, but called God's prophet a liar. They disobeyed God and moved to Egypt. The Lord told Jeremiah that Nebuchadnezzar would surely find them there and kill them (Jer. 43).

The Pharisees and Herodians. These men called Jesus a teacher of the truth, but asked questions only to trap Him, not so that they might obey (Matt. 22:15-17).

Simon the sorcerer. Simon offered Peter and John money if they would give him the Holy Spirit. Peter rebuked him for desiring the Spirit for his own selfish interests (Acts 8:18-24).

The Ethiopian eunuch. Philip shared the Word of God with this man, who immediately obeyed in repentance and faith and requested to be baptized (Acts 8:31-36).

Prayer of Application

Lord God, help me to study Your Word diligently and always with the motive of obedience to it. I pray that my lack of faith will not inhibit the Spirit's work in teaching me wisdom.

Let the Word of God Sink In

The wise in heart accept commands, but a chattering fool comes to ruin (**Prov. 10:8**).

At one time Bob was in the home-building business in California and Florida. Soil conditions, which are important in designing foundations for homes, vary widely. Compaction tests are needed to determine the soil's ability to bear weight. Drainage is necessary to carry water away from the home, so percolation tests measure the ability of the soil to drain water down into the ground.

In Florida, the sandy soils on which he built homes percolated water so fast that the soils-engineer's instruments couldn't measure it. The soil "accepts" the water quickly. But in Southern California, where the composition of the soil tends to be decomposed granite and clay, percolation may be very, very slow.

People's hearts are like soils, as we're told by Jesus in Luke 8:5-8. Some hearts receive the Word and, like water on sand, it sinks deep. This person grows in the Word and becomes sound in the faith. She becomes obedient to the indwelling Word.

The chattering fool is just the opposite. She may be continually exposed to the Word, but it runs off her mind without ever getting to her heart. She may even chatter on about her creeds and doctrines and theology, but without any real evidence in her life of the indwelling presence of the Word as applied by the Spirit of God. As the proverb anticipates, such a person will come to ruin.

Scriptural Examples

The Thessalonians. Paul thanked God for those who had received the Word of God which had gone to work in their hearts through faith (1 Thess. 2:13).

Diotrephes. This malicious person, a chattering fool, was opposing the apostle John and refusing even to welcome brothers in the faith. John said that his evil actions indicated that he had not seen God (3 John 9-11).

Prayer of Application

Dear Lord, thank You for godly pastors and teachers who feed me with the truth of Your Word. But hearing isn't enough. Help me to allow the Word to penetrate deep into my soul.

Beware of a Spiritual Stiff Neck

A man who remains stiff-necked after many rebukes will suddenly be destroyed—without remedy (**Prov. 29:1**).

Amy's parents are chiropractors, and they have seen many a stiff neck over the years. But the spiritual stiff neck is not the result of sleeping in a contorted fashion—it is the result of *living* that way. Its remedy is not chiropractic help or a muscle relaxant, but repentance and submission to the Lord.

God is very "gracious and compassionate, slow to anger and abounding in love, a God who relents from sending calamity" (Jonah 4:2). Because He is the God of "many rebukes," some think that He lacks the power or the resolve to punish sin. As Paul says, people show "contempt for the riches of [God's] kindness, tolerance and patience, not realizing that [God's] kindness leads [them] toward repentance" (Rom. 2:4). The "rebukes" in this verse are manifestations of God's kindness. But His kindness has its limits.

Women who call yourself Christian, are you living in sin? Are you consistently violating God's commandments? Know that God is not mocked, that He will not allow your sin to continue, but will visit His quick and sure discipline upon you. Your loss, even though perhaps not of salvation itself, will be eternal, and also beyond recapture (1 Cor. 3:15).

Scriptural Examples

The people of Israel. The Bible is full of examples of their backsliding and hardness of heart. The Lord even calls them "stiff-necked" in Exodus 32:9. But the nation of Israel foreshadows the church, and so we, too, need to beware that we do not fall after the example of their rebellion (Heb. 3:7-15).

The people of Nineveh. How different were these Gentiles, who, upon hearing a few sermons by that stiff-necked prophet Jonah, humbled themselves in sackcloth and ashes and softened their necks in repentance and faith (Jonah 3:6-10).

Prayer of Application

Father, You have called those who have trusted Christ for salvation to a life of obedience. Help me, Lord, by the power of Your Spirit, to live that life. Help me also to teach it to others.

Obey God's Wisdom and Live at Peace

For the waywardness of the simple will kill them, and the
complacency of fools will destroy them; but whoever listens
to me will live in safety and be at ease, without fear of harm
(**Prov. 1:32-33**).

Here are the two marks of the foolish woman. First, she is
disobedient to the light that God has given her. She is self-willed.
This path will kill her, even as God has promised that the "wages
of sin is death" (Rom. 6:23). Second, she is complacent, or self-
content. She has no need of a Savior. She thinks she's basically a
good person whom God will gladly welcome into heaven.

But God's wisdom is diametrically opposed to this simpleton's.
God demands absolute righteousness of everyone. But how can a
perfect, just, and holy God have fellowship with us when we all
bear the stain of sin? Only by God's grace. The woman who obeys
God's wisdom has her sins removed and God's righteousness
imputed to her as a gift of grace through Jesus Christ (Rom. 5:17).

This imputed righteousness restores fellowship between per-
sons and their Creator. Jesus Christ came to earth to reconcile us
to the Father by "making peace through his blood, shed on the
cross" (Col. 1:20; Eph. 2:15). We who have been saved by grace
alone through faith need not fear harm (Luke 12:4-5).

Scriptural Examples

The home builders. One man built on the rock of God's
wisdom. His house was secure even when the floods came. The
other built on the shifting sands of man's wisdom. The onrushing
waters brought disaster (Matt. 7:24-27).

The rich young ruler. This man trusted in his self-righteous-
ness. He claimed that he kept the Law of Moses, but Jesus
discerned that he loved the riches of this world more than the true
riches of God. The man rejected Jesus' advice and went sadly on
his way to destruction (Matt. 19:22).

Prayer of Application

Dear God, thank You for imputing my sins to Christ and His
righteousness to me. Without the cross there would be no fellowship with You, only a fearful expectation of the wrath to come.

Study Questions and Projects

1) Read Matthew 26:39. Who is speaking? What are the circumstances of the prayer? What is the final decision in verse 42? How should these verses influence us toward a life of submission?

2) In 1 Corinthians 16:7, Paul recognizes limits on his activities. What are they? By whom are the limits set? Does Paul react negatively to the restrictions?

3) What promises were made by God to the Israelites in Exodus 19:5-6 if they would submit to His commands? What application can we make of these verses to the Christian?

4) Read Psalm 119. On a separate sheet of paper, list all the benefits you can find for the person that obeys God. Compare your list with those of others.

5) How many masters does Christ say we can serve in Matthew 6:24? Why? What application does this verse have for your life?

6) Read 1 John 5:2-3. How does John tell us that we know God? What does verse 3 say about how difficult this is to do?

7) Meditate on Proverbs 3:5-6. What do these verses say about dual masters? About trusting and obeying God?

Other Verses to Study
Isaiah 1:19; John 14:15 and 15:10; 1 Peter 1:14;
1 John 3:22; Revelation 22:7.

One to Memorize
The wise in heart accept commands,
but a chattering fool comes to ruin (Prov. 10:8).

My Personal Action Plan to Be a Woman of Submission

1) _____ 2) _____

3) _____ 4) _____

- **Proverbs 31:24** -
*She makes linen garments and sells them,
and supplies the merchants with sashes.*

Chapter Sixteen

A Woman of Faith
• •

"Now faith is being sure of what we hope for and certain of what we do not see" (Heb. 11:1). Notice in the Hebrews verse that faith deals in things hoped for—things in the future—and things that are unseen. Faith is being sure of the future and certain of what we can't see. The wisdom woman of Proverbs 31 expressed her faith in sewing together linen garments in hope of buyers who were yet to be seen. She "knew" she would sell them. That is, she had "faith" that she would sell them, so she stitched the outfits together on the basis of that faith. Of course, the Bible is concerned primarily with the *object* of our faith: Jesus Christ.

A woman may have faith that the ice of a frozen lake is thick enough to support her as she walks across it. Suppose she begins her trek by faith, but as she gets to the middle of the lake she hears a loud "crack!"—as she slips beneath the freezing waters. She had faith. That was not her problem. Her problem was with the *object* of her faith. The ice was weak, when she had supposed it to be strong. All faith, other than faith in the One True God—our Lord Jesus Christ—is misplaced. Only He is ultimately worthy of our faith.

As you study the next proverbs, ask yourself how faith in Christ can help you to pass by the "frozen lakes" of this world that promise safety but often deliver just the opposite.

Walk by Faith, Not by Sight

***The house of the wicked will be destroyed, but the tent of the upright will flourish* (Prov. 14:11).**

The natural woman sees the things of this earth as her inheritance, so she builds her house on that foundation. She settles down and seeks to satisfy all the desires of her heart in earthly things. In the end, her house will be overthrown (Matt. 7:24-27).

The spiritual woman, on the other hand, sees herself as a stranger and a wanderer on the earth. She is looking for a better country (Heb. 11:16), a heavenly one. She doesn't build a house but lives in a tent, waiting for a home with a better foundation. By faith, she lays up possessions that she will not see until after death.

The natural woman views the spiritual woman with contempt. She mocks with words like: "How can you be so sure?" and "You're living in a dream world!" In a way, the natural woman has a point. Although our faith is sure, there is no *absolute* proof that we will ever inherit our great hope. That is why we walk by faith, toward an unseen and future hope (Heb. 11:1). Without such faith, it is impossible to please God (Heb. 11:6). Walk by faith, not by sight.

Scriptural Examples

Noah and the pre-Flood people. Noah built an ark to the scorn of the people. They trusted in the earth and its ability to provide for them, and were wicked in all their thoughts (Gen. 6:5). Noah had faith in God and was saved with his family, while those wicked people and their houses were destroyed (Gen. 6:7-8).

Pharaoh and Moses. Pharaoh was blinded to the power of God through the hardness of his heart. Moses had little earthly power, but trusted in God and walked by faith. The house of the wicked Pharaoh was destroyed (Ex. 6–14).

Jericho and Joshua. Joshua and the Israelites obeyed God and walked around Jericho for seven days before its fortress walls crumbled. Theirs was truly a walk of faith (Josh. 6:1-20).

Prayer of Application

Father, grant me the grace to walk as Abraham, Moses, Joshua, and all the other great men and women of faith. Keep my eyes fixed on Jesus, the Author and Perfector of my faith.

Put Your Trust in the Enduring Word of God

The eyes of the Lord keep watch over knowledge, but he frustrates the words of the unfaithful (**Prov.** 22:12).

Jesus said that "Heaven and earth will pass away, but my words will never pass away" (Matt. 24:35; Mark 13:31; Luke 21:33). By God's omniscience—His watchful eye—not one "jot" or one "tittle" will pass from the Word of God until all is fulfilled (Matt. 5:18), nor until heaven and earth disappear. Jesus confirms that the Lord will "keep watch over knowledge."

Down through the ages, the Bible has come under more attacks than any other document in human history. Yet it has survived those ravages with a degree of accuracy unsurpassed by any other document. *How* this has happened is a worthy study for everyone, but *why* it happened is no mystery. God has kept watch over it for His eternal purposes (Ps. 119:152). He has not allowed sinful mankind to have his way with it.

In Isaiah 55:11 God said that the word that goes out of His mouth would not return void, but that it would accomplish the purpose for which it was sent. One of God's purposes was to save both of us. We trust that one of those purposes was to save you, too, dear reader. For each of us who names the name of Christ has been "born again," not of perishable seed, but of imperishable, through the "living and enduring Word of God" (1 Pet. 1:23). This is the icing on the cake, the final proof of the pudding. Besides our objective knowledge of the truth of the Word, we know its truth subjectively because God's Spirit makes it real to us.

The unfaithful, however, are like the grass of the field. They wither and fall, "but the Word of the Lord stands forever" (1 Pet. 1:24-25; Isa. 40:6-8). Secular skeptics may try to disavow the Bible in their vain philosophies and their attempts to explain it away by naturalistic reason, but God will frustrate their every word. Only His Word is perfect. Trust only in the perfect and enduring Word of God.

Prayer of Application

Sovereign Lord, thank You for Your enduring Word. Its truth is a lamp unto my feet and a light unto my path. I pray that the Word will accomplish Your purposes through me.

Be Strongly Grounded in Your Faith

*A simple man believes anything, but a prudent man
gives thought to his steps* (Prov. 14:15).

The Christian faith is not a blind faith. It is a faith based on
solid historic fact that is backed up by the testimony of eyewit-
nesses and millions of believers down through the centuries. It is
a faith grounded in truth that was recorded in God's Word over
thousands of years by various authors, yet with one basic message
and no contradictions or errors. Furthermore, the Bible has a
quality called "perspicuity." That is, its basic doctrines are essen-
tially clear and understandable by anyone who wants to diligently
study it and seek its truth (2 Tim. 3:16).

The simple woman is tossed to and fro by every wind of
doctrine, and by the cunning craftiness of deceitful people (Eph.
4:14). Be careful not to let this happen to you. Prayerfully ground
your faith in the lifelong study of the Word. It is a book that is
sufficient for life and doctrine and does not need any other book
or priesthood to interpret it. Consider carefully each doctrine you
hear and discern whether or not it is true by testing it against the
entire revealed word of God. Be cautious of the teachers you follow
and of the church you join. Build your profession of faith on the
solid rock of God's Word, not on the shifting sand of another
person's opinion (Matt. 7:24-27).

Scriptural Examples

Eve. Acting out of emotion and self-will, rather than in faith
in what God had said, Eve was beguiled by Satan and ate the
forbidden fruit. Her rebellion started, as rebellion always does,
with a questioning of the revealed Word of God (Gen. 3:1-6).

Timothy. Paul commended Timothy, who from infancy had
known the Holy Scriptures. Those Scriptures are able to make one
wise unto salvation and are useful in equipping every person for
God's purposes (2 Tim. 3:14-17).

Prayer of Application

Father, how I love Your Word, which is trustworthy and true
and sufficient, and which is profitable in all ways for my life and
walk with You. Help me to be firmly established in it.

Please the Lord by Your Faith

When a man's ways are pleasing to the Lord, he makes even his enemies to live at peace with him (Prov. 16:7).

How do we please the Lord? We do it by faith. We must believe God exists, and that He rewards those who diligently seek Him (Heb. 11:6). Faith that pleases God is an obedient faith (James 1:22), a faith that moves out and does something because God *said* to do it. Believe on the Lord Jesus Christ, then obey His commandments and follow His ways. That faith pleases God and causes one's enemies to live at peace.

Jesus, however, said that we would be persecuted for our faith (Matt. 5:11). A person's enemies would be in his own household (Matt. 10:36). But God restrains even these enemies, and they can do no more to the believer than what God chooses to allow. In the ultimate sense, even the evil murder of a saint of God is an act that works to the saint's greater welfare. For as Paul tells us in Philippians 1:21, to die would be great gain for any believer.

Whatever your circumstances, whether your enemies are at peace with you or in outright warfare, remember that all circumstances of your life are conforming you to the image of Christ (Rom. 8:28-29), who has preceded you in death and bodily resurrection (Heb. 6:19-20). All of the saints who are in Christ have this hope as the anchor for their souls.

Scriptural Examples

Esau. Esau forgot his enmity against his brother Jacob and embraced him upon his return to the land (Gen. 33:4).

Israel. God required Israel's men to go up and worship three times a year, but promised that while they were away from home, no other nation would attack their land (Ex. 34:23-24).

Job. God put a hedge around Job and his household. He wouldn't let him be harmed by the power of Satan without the prior approval of God Himself (Job 1:9-12).

Prayer of Application

Father, may my ways please You. May the faith that You have given me continue to grow, and may I live my life by that faith so that even my enemies will live at peace with me.

Live Uprightly by Faith

*The way of the sluggard is blocked with thorns, but the path of
the upright is a highway* (Prov. 15:19).

In the Western U.S., there is a common hedge called a "natal
plum." Its thorns are very sharp. The sluggard, lacking faith, grows
in her own mind a barrier—like the natal plum—that hinders her
from seeing life as a highway. At Kadesh Barnea, God sent twelve
spies into the Promised Land. Although they liked what they saw,
ten of the spies grew such a hedge in their minds. The people grew
hedges, too. By their unbelief in the power of God, they refused to
go in and take the land. Only Caleb, Joshua, and a few others
believed that God would give them the victory (Num. 13:30).

The faithful woman's path is not an easy one, but it is a
highway not blocked by a fear that enslaves. Notice that the
proverb speaks of the "upright" and not the "diligent." The
upright woman follows her Lord's commands. She continues
steadfast in prayer, to which she expects an answer. The upright
woman believes God, and acts upon His Word without delay. To
call a woman "upright" is to claim diligence for her as well.

Scriptural Examples

The wife and mother of Proverbs. As we have seen, she was
faithful, overseeing her domain with diligence (Prov. 31:27).

The Sodomites. God condemned this wicked city, noted for
its evil, arrogance, and apathy (Ezek. 16:48-50).

The slothful and diligent servants. The lazy servant buried his
talent, but the faithful servants, entrusted with more, diligently
put their master's money to work (Matt. 25:24-30).

Some Thessalonians. Paul said that he heard of some among
them who were slothful, disorderly busybodies. He rebuked them
for their lack of diligence (2 Thess. 3:10-12).

The young widows. Paul criticized the young widows in the
church who were gossips and busy bodies (1 Tim. 5:11-14).

Prayer of Application

Dear Lord, keep me on the path of faith. I humbly ask for Your
leadership, and the strength to follow You. Let me not build up a
hedge of unbelief that blocks the highway before me.

Do Not Forget God's Deliverance

Do not lie in wait like an outlaw against a righteous man's house,
do not raid his dwelling place; for though a righteous man falls
seven times, he rises again, but the wicked are brought
down by calamity (**Prov. 24:15-16**).

Have you ever experienced trouble so deep that you could see no avenue of escape? If so, you were exactly where God wanted you to be. In such times, God reveals His mighty power.

Back in the 1970's, Bob was in Florida preparing to build homes on some golf course lots. As he was about to take out building permits, interest rates began to rise. Seeing trouble ahead, he decided to sell the lots and move his family back to California immediately. He stayed behind and settled into a lonely house. Several months went by and the lots went into foreclosure. He had only two weeks before the bank took them back. As he sat in that big empty house, lonely, frightened, and sad, Bob prayed. His back was to the wall.

Suddenly, the phone rang. On the other end was an investment banker in Los Angeles whom Bob knew slightly. His wealthy aunt had called him with a desire to buy some Florida lots. She had specified that they had to be on a golf course! Bob flew to L.A. the next day, and the deal was closed in less than two weeks.

We've each had our backs to the wall more times than seven (v. 16). Every time, God has delivered us. We pray that we've both learned more of His wisdom and will not back up to that wall again.

Scriptural Examples

The many examples. Men like Joseph, David, Gideon, and Paul, and women like Esther, Ruth, Rahab, and Mary are examples of those whose backs were to the wall, yet who experienced God's deliverance. On the other hand, many in the Bible found only calamity. The Bible is full of examples like Haman, Sennacherib, Jezebel, and Michal. Trust in God and remember His deliverances. He'll do it again and again.

Prayer of Application

Dear Lord, thank You for the many times that You have picked me up after I have stumbled and fallen. Thank You for Your rescue from the ultimate peril I face: death and judgment.

Study Questions and Projects

1) Read the following Old Testament verses and write a brief description of how faith was exemplified in each. Use a separate sheet of paper if necessary.

      a) Genesis 6:22 - _____

      b) Genesis 50:20 - _____

      c) Exodus 15:2 - _____

      d) 1 Samuel 14:6 - _____

      e) 1 Samuel 17:37 - _____

      f) 2 Samuel 7:28 - _____

      g) Nehemiah 2:20 - _____

      h) Job 13:15 - _____

      i) Psalm 3:3-6 - _____

      j) Psalm 13:5 - _____

      k) Habakkuk 3:17-18 - _____

2) What lesson about faith is Christ teaching in Matthew 7:24-27? What illustration does He use?

3) What effect does faith have on our salvation according to John 1:12? John 3:16? John 5:24? John 11:25? John 20:31?

4) Read 2 Corinthians 5:7. With what does Paul contrast faith? What are the effects of saving faith in your life?

Other Verses to Study

Psalm 121:2; Galatians 2:20; Ephesians 2:8-9; 2 Timothy 1:12.

One to Memorize

The eyes of the Lord keep watch over knowledge, but he frustrates the words of the unfaithful (Prov. 22:12).

My Personal Action Plan to Be a Woman of Faith

1) _____ 2) _____

3) _____ 4) _____

- Proverbs 31:25 -
She is clothed with strength and dignity;
she can laugh at the days to come.

Chapter Seventeen

A Woman Who Knows God

· ·

Faith in Christ is a wonderful thing to have. But, the big question is, faith in *which* Christ? Jesus said, "Many will come in my name, claiming, 'I am the Christ,' and will deceive many" (Matt. 24:5). Jesus was speaking about false prophets who would preach a different Christ and a different gospel: those whom Paul condemns in Galatians 1:6-8. How can we know for sure that we are following the true Christ?

God has given us His Word and He has commanded that we study it and master it (2 Tim. 2:15). Jesus says that it is the Bible that testifies about Him (John 5:39). The knowledge of our true Savior and God is not just essential in our salvation but in every detail of our lives. How will we live for Him, worship Him, obey Him and delight Him, if we do not know who He is? The Word of God is our window into the person of God. Only through His distinct revelation of Himself can we truly know Him.

Once we know God, we can truly "laugh at the days to come." Our security is wrapped up in Christ, so we can relax and enjoy Him. The Proverbs 31 woman was clothed in strength, dignity, and joy from knowing her Savior. We who are clothed in His righteousness can share her peace.

Don't Worry, God Is in Control

*In his heart a man plans his course, but the Lord
determines his steps* (Prov. 16:9).

Do people have free will? We do indeed have freedom of choice, for God could not hold us responsible for our decisions if we did not. And yet humans can do nothing to thwart the purposes of God. We may make our plans, but in the final analysis it is God's will that will be done (Matt. 6:10). How different this concept is from the popular song that says God is "watching us from a distance." Many believe in a kind of "dualism" in which Satan is free of the absolute control of God. But even Satan is a mere creature, subject to God's control.

God, who is all-powerful and all-seeing, directs the course of mankind's free will to achieve His own eternal purposes. If that were not so, He would cease to be God, and would assume the role of some cringing husbandman, wringing his hands in the fear that history would not turn out the way He wanted.

Because God sits enthroned in power over the events of the universe and the circumstances of our everyday lives, it is the obligation of every Christian to trust Him for the future. We are to rest from worry, which is sin. Our God is in absolute control.

Scriptural Examples

King Xerxes. Because of his sleepless night, the plot by Haman against Mordecai and the Jews was foiled. You guessed it! It was God who caused his sleeplessness (Est. 6:1).

Philip. Philip had been preaching to many in Samaria when the Spirit told him to go to a eunuch in the desert. God predetermined the encounter, but Philip chose to obey (Acts 8:26-40).

Onesimus. This slave ran away from his master, Philemon, but his steps led right into the arms of Christ via the apostle Paul. Later, Onesimus returned to his master, but this time as his brother in the Lord (the book of Philemon).

Prayer of Application

Father, I pray that I may plan according to the leading of Your Spirit. But I know that You will use even my sin to Your great glory. Thank You for giving me confidence in Your providence.

Live a Joyful Life Under the Gaze of God

The eyes of the Lord are everywhere, keeping watch on the wicked and the good (Prov. 15:3).

The natural person rebels at the notion that God sees every detail of her life. This fact shouldn't surprise the Bible student. We see it in the Garden of Eden immediately following the Fall when Adam and Eve tried to hide from their Creator, covering their nakedness with leaves (Gen. 3:7-10). But God has perfect knowledge. There is no escape from His constant gaze.

But we who have been reconciled to God through Christ (Eph. 4:24) should have no fear in standing naked before Him. He is our great High Priest who cleanses our defilements and covers us, as He did the first couple, with righteous garments (Heb. 4:13-14). Dr. R. C. Sproul calls us to live our lives "Coram Deo," which is Latin for, "under God's gaze." For the child of God, the gaze is no threat. Conversely, it is a promise of safekeeping, that God will keep us in His tender care and work out all of the circumstances of our lives to His great glory and our eternal benefit (Rom. 8:28-29).

Scriptural Examples

Hagar. Mistreated by Sarai and left alone in the desert, Hagar was comforted by God's angel. She gave God the name that in English means "You are the God who sees me" (Gen. 16:6-15).

Moses and the people of Israel. At the burning bush Jehovah told Moses that He had seen His people's suffering in the land of Egypt and had heard their cries of anguish (Ex. 3:7).

Gehazi. Elisha's servant sought to profit secretly from Naaman's healing. God, through Elisha, accused Gehazi and transferred Naaman's leprosy to him (2 Kings 5:19-27).

Nathanael. Jesus displayed his omniscience by telling Nathanael where he saw him, sitting under the branches of a fig tree. Nathanael, because of this miracle of Jesus' omniscience, recognized Jesus as the promised Messiah (John 1:48-49).

Prayer of Application

Lord, may the knowledge of Your constant gaze into my life purify me from sin, comfort me in times of trouble, and bring me the joy that only comes from loving Your mighty power.

Worship God in His Sovereignty

The lot is cast into the lap, but its every decision is from the Lord
(Prov. 16:33).

Some Christians think of God as a disinterested observer of this world. Others view Him as a sort of glorified errand boy who is waiting to serve their every whim. But the biblical picture of God is as Sovereign Lord, who is working out His purposes in the history of this planet in detail.

Historians can't tell us much about the "lot" in terms of what it looked like, but its purpose was to aid in making decisions. We've always envisioned a pair of dice when we hear the term "lot." The dice players in Las Vegas say, "Luck be a lady tonight." But the Bible teaches that there is no such thing as "luck."

While we don't know much about the lot, there exists today a better way for good decision-making. First, let's seek to know the Word of God (2 Peter 1:19). Then, let's trust fully in the One who wrote it (Prov. 3:5-6), resting in His providential care. Next, we need to seek the godly advice of others. Finally, let's make our decisions and step out by faith in the sovereignty of the One who created and sustains all things by His powerful Word (Heb. 1:3). Let us worship God by faithfully resting in Him.

Scriptural Examples

Joseph. He was cast into a pit by his brothers at precisely the same time a caravan of Ishmaelites went by. Joseph wound up as a slave in Egypt. Later, in power there, Joseph told his brothers that they had meant his slavery for evil, but God had intended it for good—to save many lives (Gen. 37:25; 45:4-8).

Jonah. The sailors on the ship carrying Jonah cast lots to see who was responsible for the storm that threatened their ship. The lot fell upon Jonah, so they cast him into the sea at precisely the same time that a great fish, which God had prepared, swam by and swallowed him. Luck? No way! (Jonah 1:7).

Prayer of Application

Father, help me always to rest in You. Your power to control every detail of Your creation is too high for me to understand, but by faith I can find my rest in it, and please You.

In Discipline, Find the Father's Love

My son, do not despise the Lord's discipline and do not resent his rebuke, because the Lord disciplines those he loves, as a father the son he delights in (**Prov.** 3:11-12).

Have you ever heard someone say, "Come to Jesus, and all your problems will be solved"? That is very misleading. Nowhere are we told that we will not have problems on this earth. In fact, Jesus says, "You will have trouble" (John 16:33). Bob didn't have extensive earthly trouble until he became a Christian at age 33. He wondered, "Why doesn't God just take me home and spare me from this?" Since then, he's discovered that God keeps us here, in part, to make us into the person He wants us to be. We are disciplined for our good, as children beloved by the Father (Heb. 12:5-11).

God disciplines those He loves in two ways. One way is through His hand. Amy says that she learned much about God from His disciplining hand—not the recommended way. If you get away with sin—without repentance—and do not experience God's discipline, you should tremble, because you are very likely an illegitimate child and not a true child (Heb. 12:8). There is a better way.

The best way to find the Father's discipline is by the study and memorization of His Word (Ps. 119:11). Scripture is given to us by God to train us in godliness (2 Tim. 3:16), and to cause us to grow to maturity in Christ (Heb. 5:14). By either path, God will get you where He wants you to go; but believe us, the latter is the much more pleasant route.

Scriptural Examples

The Laodicean church. This lukewarm church was rebuked by Christ for its lack of commitment. They were neither cold nor hot, and He threatened to spit them out of His mouth. He stood at the door of their hearts and knocked. Those who were Christians would hear His voice and open the door, receiving His discipline, and the joy of His subsequent fellowship (Rev. 3:14-20).

Prayer of Application

Lord, thank You for Your hand of discipline, as You guide me into Your truth through Your Word or by Your fearsome hand. If I leave the path, You will turn me back to the true way.

Beware of Your Innate Independence

The king's heart is in the hand of the Lord; he directs it like a watercourse wherever he pleases (Prov. 21:1).

East of our home, the mountains drop quickly into the Imperial Valley. Much of this parched desert land was transformed into a garden earlier in this century by the introduction of irrigation canals. Now, farmers water their fields simply by opening and closing gates in water ditches. This is the picture we have in the verse above. God opens and closes gates directing the king's water into the fields of God's own choosing.

It is a very appropriate illustration in another sense as well. The flow of the water is naturally under the control of the king. The liberty of his own ability to choose is not impaired by God. He is responsible for all of his actions. But the results of those actions belong to God. Notice that God is directing the *course* of the water, not its *flow*. And what more forceful illustration than that of a king's heart, the most absolute of all earthly volitions!

Dr. J. Vernon McGee once pointed out that in America we have a Declaration of Independence, but today it seems to be used to declare our independence from God. People seek to do whatever pleases them. But if the King of kings directs the ordinary king's watercourse, will He not also direct the steps of everyone on earth? What we need in America, Dr. McGee stated, is a "Declaration of Dependence" upon the Living and True God. Watch your own sinful desire to be independent of God. Trust in the One who controls the direction of all things.

Scriptural Examples

The kings. The Bible is full of kings. There are good kings and bad kings, honest kings and lying kings, godly kings and wicked kings. But all of these men have one thing in common. Each one fulfilled the purposes of Almighty God, whether that was his express intention or not (Rev. 17:16-17).

Prayer of Application

Father, it is a mystery how I have moral responsibility for my choices, and yet You direct all results by your providential oversight. Help me to trust fully in Your divine power.

Live in Absolute Dependence upon God

A man's steps are directed by the Lord. How then can anyone understand his own way? (**Prov. 20:24**).

Because we were born under the curse of sin, we want to be in control. We want to be the "master of our fate, the captain of our soul." The notion of a holy God who controls our every step is unthinkable. Though God works through us, many Christians perceive of God depending upon *us*, not the other way around. But God's Word tells us that we are absolutely helpless apart from Him. God is *the* "mover and shaker." There is no other.

Ironically, for the woman who understands the absolute sovereignty of God, it is her "Magna Carta" of freedom. It is *not* a freedom to sin. God forbid! It is a freedom from worry, from fear and anxiety, from the false guilt of legalism, and from the necessity *to* sin. Are we free from personal responsibility? No. Our dependence does not imply passivity, but rather a call to diligence without presumption. When a Christian sins deliberately, she presumes upon our Lord's grace. May we never do that!

We challenge you to cast off any world view that opposes the absolute sovereignty of God. Let the Bible speak to you, and then prostrate yourself before God in absolute dependence upon His mighty power and grace.

Scriptural Examples

Rebekah. She just "happened" to come out of her house at precisely the same time that Eliezer finished praying that God would deliver to him Isaac's wife-to-be (Gen. 24:12-15).

Pharaoh's daughter. This woman just "happened" to be at the Nile when Moses was hidden. Then she just "happened" to select Moses' real mother as his nursemaid (Ex. 2:1-9).

Rehoboam. This young king's heart was turned against the people's advice. Why? It was to fulfill the word of God as spoken to Jereboam through Ahijah (1 Kings 12:1-15).

Prayer of Application

Sovereign Lord, help me to understand clearly that You sustain my every breath. Thank You that—by Your grace—You reached down and saved me while I was yet your bitter enemy.

Study Questions and Projects

1) What do the following Old Testament verses tell us about who our God is? Write down a brief answer in the space provided.

    a) Genesis 1:1 - _____

    b) Genesis 17:1 - _____

    c) Exodus 40:34-35 - _____

    d) Ruth 1:6 - _____

    e) Job 37:5 - _____

    f) Psalm 27:11 - _____

    g) Psalm 33:5 - _____

    h) Psalm 33:11 - _____

    i) Psalm 37:28 - _____

    j) Psalm 68:5 - _____

    k) Psalm 90:1-2 - _____

    l) Isaiah 6:3 - _____

    m) Isaiah 46:9-10 - _____

    n) Isaiah 54:8 - _____

    o) Jeremiah 23:24 - _____

    p) Lamentations 3:37 - _____

2) How should the knowledge you have acquired through these verses help to change your life? Discuss with others.

Other Verses to Study
Psalm 117:2; 139:3-10; John 4:24 and 17:3; 1 Timothy 1:17.

One to Memorize
The king's heart is in the hand of the Lord; he directs it like a watercourse wherever he pleases (Prov. 21:1).

My Personal Action Plan to Be a Woman Who Knows God

1) _____ 2) _____

3) _____ 4) _____

- Proverbs 31:26 -
She speaks with wisdom,
and faithful instruction is on her tongue.

Chapter Eighteen

A Woman Who Speaks Wisely

• •

A number of proverbs address the issue of the tongue. Slander, gossip, false witness, lies, anger and bitterness, violence, perverseness, and conceit are some of its fruits. Proverbs 13:3 says, "He who guards his lips guards his life." The woman of Proverbs 31 is someone like that. She "speaks with wisdom, and faithful instruction."

Another Bible writer who addressed the problems associated with the tongue was James. He says, "If anyone is never at fault in what he says, he is a perfect man, able to keep his whole body in check" (James 3:2). The tongue is the fountain out of which our heart pours. In other words, *who we are* will be clearly seen by *what we say.*

Think back to when you were in high school. Were you ever "put down" by someone you thought was a friend? Although it hurt you at the time, it hurt your detractor's reputation more. It showed her insecurity and shallowness. By putting you down, she sought to elevate herself in the eyes of others. It's a cheap and pitiful way of life, much like the perennial critic who seeks to elevate her intellectual status by knocking the ideas of others.

But the way of wisdom seeks to elevate others at the expense of self. We recommend that you study all of the proverbs that deal with speaking, so that you, too, will "speak with wisdom."

Fight with Patience and a Gentle Tongue

Through patience a ruler can be persuaded, and a gentle tongue can break a bone (Prov. 25:15).

Back in the days of Napoleon and the French Revolution, when heads were rolling and blood was flowing in the streets of Paris, a man across the English Channel was waging a different kind of warfare. His name was William Wilberforce, and his enemy was the English slave trade. For over forty years this devout Christian politician exercised patience and a gentle tongue, and won the battle to emancipate all of the slaves in the British Empire. What a contrast to the blood that flowed in America's Civil War, that was fought over this same issue. And what a contrast to the way we people of this world typically wage our little wars!

Our minds seem to go instinctively to 1 Peter 3:1-2 when we think of this proverb. There, women who are married to unbelievers are given instructions about how they are to graciously live with their husbands. Peter might just as well have quoted this proverb, applying it to unbelieving husbands. Nagging and belittling and arguing over doctrine never won anybody to the Lord. But patience and a gentle tongue have persuaded many.

Let us follow Christ's example, and whether the battle that rages around you is in your home, at your job, in your school, or at your church, use the weapons of patience and a gentle tongue. God is in control.

Scriptural Examples

David and Saul. While Saul was waging war with the tools of the world, David used a gentle tongue. At one juncture, Saul killed eighty-five priests of God in his vehement wrath. But twice when he had Saul cornered, David refused to take his life. Instead, David spoke to him with patience and gentleness. Saul was forced to confess, "May you be blessed, my son David." And David *was* blessed (1 Sam. 24:8-20; 26:17-25).

Prayer of Application

Dear God, I am often tempted to raise my voice in anger when confronted with wickedness in the world. Help me instead to use the weapons of patience and a gentle tongue.

Respect the Dignity of Others

A man who lacks judgment derides his neighbor, but a man of understanding holds his tongue. A gossip betrays a confidence, but a trustworthy man keeps a secret (**Prov.** 11:12-13).

We all know people who love to hear juicy gossip and can't wait to spread it. They don't even consider whether it is true, or whether they may harm someone. They just open their mouths and out it comes. What motivates these people to act as they do?

As usual, pride is the principle culprit. A gossip wants to feel superior to her neighbor. By debasing her target, she thinks she is elevating herself. Gossip is cheap and fraudulent. The gossip may even reveal secret things that were given to her in strictest confidence, simply to gain this self-exaltation.

Gossip and slander are the safest ways to attack someone. To confront a neighbor directly is too perilous. How much safer it is to secretly sneak behind her back! We must be discerning of this foolishness and rebuke the gossip. To listen to gossip is to give credence to it. The gossip is a coward and only exhibits a low opinion of herself in her madness.

But the woman of wisdom holds her peace. Why? First, wisdom implies self-knowledge. A woman of wisdom knows that she is not superior to her neighbor. Second, wisdom brings with it the "love" principle. Love does no harm to its neighbor (Rom. 13:10). We are to love our neighbor as ourselves, and treat her with dignity. With God's help, may we act only in love.

Scriptural Examples

Tobiah and Sanballat. These evil men tried to frighten Nehemiah into thinking they were coming to kill him. They showed their lack of wisdom as they spread their lies (Neh. 6).

Judas. What a picture of gossips! They kiss you when in your presence, telling you what a fine person you are, but stab you in the back when out of earshot (Matt. 26:47-49).

Prayer of Application

Dear Lord, by Your Spirit, keep me from listening to or spreading gossip. Help me instead to live by the law of love that seeks no harm for its neighbor, aspiring only to that which is good.

Speak with Kindness

Reckless words pierce like a sword, but the tongue of the wise brings healing (Prov. 12:18).

Bob has never been pierced by a sword, but he did put a telephone pole climber's spike through his foot as a boy, and he knows the pain that is involved. It took many hours for the pain to subside. Then it left a scar. Both of us have received harsh words from a loved one that put a pain in our chest like that of a sword.

Teachers can inflict pain on children with words. Conversely, gentle encouragement can make a child soar to the heights. Mothers, realize the impact your words have on your little ones, as well as others in your family.

God calls us to kindness (Gal. 5:22). Our first consideration must always be for the glory of God, and then for the welfare of others (Matt. 22:36-40). God has treated us with incredible kindness. How then can we treat other human beings with anything but the same? Shall we not rebuke others? Yes, we must rebuke them when necessary, but in kindness, hoping for reconciliation between parties, and growth for all (2 Cor. 2:5-7).

Scriptural Examples

Jesus. Our Lord was often the recipient of reckless words. Because He associated with people of low estate and attended banquets and parties, the Jewish leaders falsely said of Him, "Here is a glutton and a drunkard" (Matt. 11:19).

Jesus. As He stood before the Sanhedrin, and testified truthfully of Himself, He was falsely called a blasphemer (Mark 14:64).

Jesus. They accused Him also of sedition (Luke 23:5) and of anarchy in plotting the destruction of the temple (Mark 14:58).

Jesus. But our Lord always spoke with kindness, except in moments of righteous rebuke (Matt. 23). Even then, His words were truthful, not slanderous. Our Lord spoke with words of comfort and encouragement. We are called to walk in His steps.

Prayer of Application

Father, thank You for Jesus, who spoke words of life and salvation. Help me, Lord, to treat all people with kindness—for Christ's sake, and because they are made in God's image.

Be an Encourager

A word aptly spoken is like apples of gold in settings of silver. Like an earring of gold or an ornament of fine gold is a wise man's rebuke to a listening ear (**Prov. 25:11-12**).

Golden apples do not grow where we live, but we do have golden oranges. However, the allusion here seems to be to apples of the precious metal gold. Perhaps they are set in a silver ring. The idea is that a word aptly spoken is like a precious and choice jewel.

Let's temporarily replace the word "rebuke" in verse 12 with "encouragement," and look at the verses in that light. Actually, rebuke *is* encouragement. When we gently rebuke someone, such as our children or an employee, our motive should be to encourage them to be their very best. So the two words are very closely related.

If you are looking for a job to do in your local congregation, why not set yourself up as president of the "Encourager's Club"? There are no dues or by-laws, and it's okay if you are the only member. All you have to do to get started is to find someone who needs encouragement, and encourage him or her! Those who you know are hurting may need a kind word and an assurance that you are standing with them. You could send notes of encouragement to the sick. Or you just might write about how you appreciate the other person. Number one on your list of "encouragees" should be your pastor and his wife. Congratulate those who have done a good job. Thank those who have selflessly given their time. Use your imagination!

Scriptural Examples

Boaz. Boaz noticed Ruth as she gleaned in his field and encouraged her to stay and gather much. He commended her for her love for Naomi, and gave her his blessing (Ruth 2:8-12).

Barnabas. This companion of Paul was a great joy to him. Even his name means "son of encouragement" (Acts 4:36).

Prayer of Application

Heavenly Father, help me to encourage others. I know from my own experience how sweet a word of encouragement is from a brother or sister. It seems to breathe new life into me.

Speak Words of Life

*From the fruit of his mouth a man's stomach is filled; with the
harvest from his lips he is satisfied. The tongue has the power of
life and death, and those who love it will eat its fruit*
(**Prov. 18:20-21**).

The old saying, "Sticks and stones may break my bones, but
words can never hurt me," is about as far from the truth as an old
saying can get. Words can be devastating, even, as we see here, unto
death. Conversely, there are words of comfort, blessing, encouragement, and life. We need to speak those.

It might be revealing for each of us to carry along a tape
recorder for a week. Wouldn't we cringe at the words we wish we
could stuff back in our mouths? Like the prophet Isaiah, most of
us would want to cry out, "I am a man of unclean lips" (Isa. 6:5).

As Christians, we have been entrusted with the true Word of
Life (Phil. 2:16). In all of our speaking we need to hold forth the
Word, so that we may know that our labor and sojourn on this
earth were not in vain, as Paul exhorts us (1 Cor. 15:58).

But how do we do it? First, we are to diligently study the Word,
making it a part of our daily life (2 Tim. 2:15). Then we need to
ask God to restrain our tongues, causing our lips to be consecrated
to the One who is *the* Life, our Lord Jesus.

Scriptural Examples

Melchizidek. This king of Salem was priest of the Most High
God. He blessed Abram on his return from defeating the kings who
had kidnapped Lot and his family. His words of blessing are
followed in the text by God's promise to Abram of a son and
offspring more numerous than the stars of the sky. God also gave
Abram the assurance of justification by grace, through faith. Surely
the blessing of Melchizidek, a type of the High Priesthood and
Kingship of Christ, were words of life to Abraham (Gen. 14:19–
15:6; Heb. 5:6-10).

Prayer of Application

Dear Lord, create in me a tongue of life, from which may flow
the blessings of the Word of God. May I seek only good for my
neighbor, that I may be a true ambassador of Christ Jesus.

Limit Your Words

When words are many, sin is not absent, but he who holds his tongue is wise (**Prov. 10:19**).

James' epistle has much to say about the tongue. He says in 1:19 that we should be quick to listen and slow to speak, and in 1:26 that if we consider ourselves to be religious, and yet do not keep a tight rein on our tongues, our religion is worthless. The tongue is a fire (3:6), corrupting a person, setting her ablaze.

Consider the analogy of the volcano. As we grow in the Word and in the control of the Holy Spirit, we undergo a gradual sanctification process. This process allows us to filter the words of our mouths through a biblical grid, which serves like a cap on Mt. Vesuvius. The old volcano deep within still seeks to blow out words of anger, sarcasm, gossip, and the like. But as we grow in Christ, we should begin to speak only suitable and profitable words of kindness, love, peace, and joy. The "old" woman in us doesn't change, but the "new" woman is given a new desire and perspective that should produce godly speech through that biblical grid.

How are we to practice reining in our wicked tongues? Before you speak, pause and ask yourself, "Is it kind? Is it true? Is it profitable? Is it necessary?" If the answer to *all* those questions is "Yes," then go ahead and speak. If not, hold your tongue.

Scriptural Examples

Miriam and Aaron. They began to speak against their brother Moses because he had taken a Cushite wife. They were also jealous of Moses' special relationship with God (Num. 12:1-9).

Job and friends. Elihu accused Job of multiplying words of emptiness (Job 35:16), and Job accused his friends of the same (Job 27:12). As usual, God had the last word (Job. 38:2; 42:7).

The praying pagans. Our Lord spoke out against those who would multiply their words in prayer, thinking they would be heard for their verbosity (Matt. 6:7-8).

Prayer of Application

Heavenly Father, thank You for delivering me from the power of sin in my life. Continue to work in me, Lord, to the end that the words of my mouth would be few and pleasing to You.

Study Questions and Projects

1) Read Psalm 12. What is David's lament in verse 1? What two things do the ungodly do in verse 2? In your own words, what does the boastful tongue say? How do God's words differ from those of the ungodly? Meditate on verse 8. In what ways is that verse true in our own time? Do some things never change?

2) In Psalm 52, David speaks of what the evil Doeg the Edomite did when he lied to Saul about David's visit to Ahimelech (1 Sam. 22:9). Of what did Doeg boast? What did Doeg love? Rather than what? What does David say will be the end of someone like this? But with what does David compare himself in verse 8? Why? How does David use his tongue?

3) Read Psalm 15. David says there are eleven things that the person who "will never be shaken" does. See if you can find all of them. Write them down, in your own words, on a separate sheet of paper. How does your life stack up against David's list?

4) Read Luke 6:45. What principle does Jesus give us here regarding the tongue? Discuss with others.

5) Paul exhorts us in Ephesians 4:22–5:8 to "put off your old self" and "put on the new self." What specific instructions does he give us for this process? How does his list compare with that of David in Psalm 15? Do you see anything new added?

Other Verses to Study
Proverbs 14:3; 15:1; 16:21; 17:27; 19:1; 26:5; and 29:11.

One to Memorize
When words are many, sin is not absent, but he who holds his tongue is wise (Prov. 10:19).

My Personal Action Plan to Be a Woman Who Speaks Wisely

1) _____ 2) _____

3) _____ 4) _____

Chapter Nineteen

A Woman of Godly Wisdom

What exactly does the word "wisdom" mean? First, there are two types of wisdom: "worldly" and "godly." The wisdom of the world is foolishness in God's sight (1 Cor. 3:19), and the wisdom of God is foolishness in the world's sight (1 Cor. 1:14). They are diametrically opposed to each other. Each seeks to "watch over the affairs of her household," that is, to live in such a way as to get the most out of life. But only one of them is the *way* to life. The other leads to death (Prov. 14:12).

The world's wisdom exalts self: the creature rather than the Creator. Paul says in Romans 1:21-23 that sinful people neither glorify God nor are thankful to Him. They profess to be *wise*, but they are fools, and exchange the glory of God for images of themselves and other creatures. The wisdom of the world seeks *independence* from the God of glory.

Conversely, the wisdom of God says to *depend* upon Him. James says such wisdom "is first of all pure; then peaceloving, considerate, submissive, full of mercy and good fruit, impartial and sincere" (3:17). The book of Proverbs has been called "the Ten Commandments in shoe-leather." It has been designed by God to give us step-by-step guidance in living with godly wisdom.

Put Your Wisdom to Practical Application

*Every prudent man acts out of knowledge, but a fool
exposes his folly* (Prov. 13:16).

It's one thing to have wisdom as mere "head knowledge," but
quite another to apply it to our lives. This is the essence of prudence.
Otherwise, such wisdom will just puff up our pride.

Practical uses for wisdom are in training our children (Judg.
13:8-12), exercising caution against pitfalls along the path (Prov.
22:3), using wise counsel in discipline (Rom. 15:14), practicing
moderation (Titus 1:8), organizing finances (Prov. 11:15 and
22:26), and in decision-making (2 Thess. 2:15-17). The spiritual
woman's wisdom is shown in her prudent walk.

Conversely, the fool is a natural at exposing her folly. Like
Balaam, she vents her wrath (Num. 22:29-30). Like Goliath, she
boasts loudly in her vanity (1 Sam. 17:44). Like Herod, she is
thoughtless in her promises (Matt. 14:7). Like Simon the Sorcerer, she'll do anything for a buck (Acts 8:9-24). Like so many
examples in Scripture, and in our experience, fools display folly.

Scriptural Examples

Abigail. Abigail showed great prudence in dealing with David
and his men and with her foolish spouse. When Nabal got drunk,
she circumspectly waited until he was sober before confronting
him with the events of the day. As it all turned out, Nabal was
"dying" to hear Abigail's words (1 Sam. 25:36-37).

Ezra. This prudent man of God stopped by a canal to pray for
a safe journey to Jerusalem. He had not wanted to ask King Xerxes
for an armed guard because he had told the king that God would
protect them. God did exactly that (Ezra 8:21-23).

Jesus. Once again our Great Example shone in His application of wisdom. He walked circumspectly to avoid His enemies
(John 11:47-54). But it was in His teaching ministry that His great
wisdom shone most clearly (Matt. 13:54).

Prayer of Application

Heavenly Father, may the prudent application of Your Word
in my life keep me from sin and error, and show others Your
marvelous grace. Help me to glorify Christ in every way.

In Wisdom, Find the Secret Things of God

By wisdom the Lord laid the earth's foundations, by understanding he set the heavens in place; by his knowledge the deeps were divided, and the clouds let drop the dew (**Prov. 3:19-20**).

If you think that the universe in all its power, majesty, orderliness, and beauty is incredible and vast, then you should read the Bible. The Word is unequaled in splendor in its revelation of the glory and plan of God. While much may be known of God through His creation (Rom. 1:20), such as His power, unity, knowledge, wisdom, and beauty, it does not speak to us of His most wonderful essence and plan.

Only through the Word do we learn of the reason why things have gone wrong in God's world. Only through the Word do we learn of God's love for us, and the gospel which is able to save us from our sin. The proverbs above point to the wisdom and understanding of God as He established the earth, as He set each star of the firmament in position, and as the seas were formed and the ecosystems set up. What a mighty God we serve!

Read the Word. Study the Word. Meditate on the Word. Memorize the Word. Share the Word with others. In it, we are given the knowledge of the secret things of God, established since the foundations of the world (Deut. 29:29).

Scriptural Examples

Job. This godly man suffered for his faithfulness at the hands of Satan. But Job knew of these secret things of God and glorified his Creator and Redeemer (Job 26).

Jesus. How often we think of Jesus as the humble little baby, the itinerant preacher and healer, or as our Savior. But He is also the great "I AM" of the burning bush (Ex. 3:14), and the El Shaddai of infinite power. The entire Bible speaks of this Word who was made flesh and dwelt among us. All history is *His* story. All wisdom is His wisdom (John 1:1-14).

Prayer of Application

Father, thank You for Your self-revelation through creation. Further, thank You for Your wonderful Word which reveals so much more. Help me to know the Word and teach it to others.

Exercise Wisdom Combined with Faith

Whoever gives heed to instruction prospers, and blessed is he who trusts in the Lord (**Prov. 16:20**).

If a woman has true wisdom, she will understand that her natural or earthly wisdom cannot alone be trusted. She will realize her dependence upon her Creator, by faith acknowledging that true instruction and wisdom comes from above (James 3:17).

And where does this heavenly wisdom lead? It leads to the qualities of Christlikeness that God desires us to exhibit. Faith leads to goodness, knowledge, self-control, perseverance, godliness, brotherly kindness, and love (2 Pet. 1:5-7).

To lean fully upon God for all of our needs, such as a child relies completely upon his parents, is the key to blessedness in this life. Where then is anxiety or worry? Where is fear? These are all cast out by God's perfect love and provision (1 John 4:18). It's not easy. As youngsters, we are encouraged to "stand on your own two feet" and be independent. Then, as new Christians, we are faced with the obligation to trust God completely, and lean not upon our own understanding (Prov. 3:5-6). It is a formidable transition, one that we have not begun to finish, but one well worth the trials engaged in its accomplishment.

Scriptural Examples

Joseph. God's wisdom in a time of national emergency, a famine, worked through this man who trusted in God's leadership. God provided for Egypt and began the formation in Egypt of what was to become the nation Israel (Gen. 41:25-44).

Ahithophel. The advice of this man was set aside by the Lord who intended to bring disaster upon Absalom. God's wisdom overcomes even the best human wisdom (2 Sam. 17:14).

The apostles. These men used godly wisdom in setting up the office of deacon to assist the widows, and then in selecting the people who would fill the office (Acts 6:1-7).

Prayer of Application

Lord God, increase my wisdom in the daily struggles that are set before me, and increase my faith and trust in Your provision for my every need. Blessed is she who rests in You.

Do Not Equate Wealth and Wisdom

A rich man may be wise in his own eyes, but a poor man who has discernment sees through him (**Prov. 28:11**).

We often elevate the rich and famous to pedestals of honor. They speak at banquets and conventions, and we come in droves to hear them, hoping that a little of their wisdom will rub off on us. Remember the smug saying, "If you're so smart, why aren't you rich"? It's as if those who possess the world's riches are models of moral excellence, far exalted above us mere mortals.

But far too often the rich woman is what she is because of greed and treachery, not because of high ethical standards and a keen sense of fair play. And even if wealth is gained in a morally upright way, does not its possessor often see herself as "self-made," independent of God? Is she not "wise in her own eyes"?

Amy's background is in non-profit development—raising money from the very wealthy. Many times, but not always, she found the wealthy women with whom she worked to be more interested in notoriety and self-exaltation than in helping the charity.

But the poor woman will not be seen on the dais of this world's society tea parties. Why? Because the world worships wealth and fame and power. The poor woman with discernment worships the One with whom the world wants no relationship.

Scriptural Examples

Naaman and his servants. Wise in his own eyes, he rejected the advice of Elisha to wash in the Jordan River in order to be healed of his leprosy. But his servants saw through his arrogance and advised him to follow Elisha's command (2 Kings 5:9-14).

The ruler of Tyre. This city was a center of commerce in the ancient world. Its prince had become "wise in his own eyes" because of the great wealth which he had amassed. He failed to honor God, who promised him a violent death in the same sea that had carried his ships with such success (Ezek. 28:1-8).

Prayer of Application

Dear Savior, I know that wealth only brings increased accountability before You. Help me to use any riches that may come my way for Your glory and honor, and not selfishly or foolishly.

Walk Prudently and Take Refuge

*A prudent man sees danger and takes refuge, but the simple keep
going and suffer for it* (Prov. 22:3).

The prudent woman will foresee difficulty in the road ahead
and plan for it. The simple woman, on the other hand, just keeps
on truckin' down the road, fearing nothing. The older we get, the
more clearly we ought to see danger ahead, but how often we are
"cockeyed optimists." Some of life's troubles may blindside us, as
when a car comes flying toward us on the wrong side. But most
problems are foreseeable if we'll just take the time to hear wise
counsel and plan ahead.

There is danger ahead in spades for many on this planet who
are walking down the road of life without God, whistling a happy
tune. It is the sure judgment and wrath of God (Heb. 9:27; Acts
17:31). There is only one refuge from His wrath—Jesus Christ. He
offers His covering and protection from the coming judgment
free-of-charge to anyone who comes to Him in faith (Isa. 55:7;
Rom. 6:23; Eph. 2:8; Rev. 22:17), trusting in His blood shed on
the cross as a sacrifice for sin. If you have never trusted Christ for
His refuge, do so today.

Scriptural Examples

Noah. Noah was warned about the flood and built a huge ship.
Meanwhile, for more than 100 years, he preached to lost souls of
the coming doom. No one came forward to set foot on the ark. The
flood came, as God said that it would, and swept them all away.
Noah's faith condemned the world and made him an heir of
righteousness (Gen. 6:9–7:12; Heb. 11:7).

The Israelites. God warned the Israelites that He would send
one final plague upon the Egyptians. Those households that had
not prepared by placing the blood of a lamb on the lintel of their
doorway would lose the firstborn son. The Israelites believed God
and escaped the danger ahead (Ex. 12).

Prayer of Application

Lord, your Word is a lamp unto my feet and a light unto my
path. Help me to see its warnings of trouble ahead and, trusting
fully in Your ability and desire to deliver me, move out in faith.

Let Christ's Wisdom Rest in Your Heart

Wisdom reposes in the heart of the discerning and even among fools she lets herself be known (**Prov. 14:33**).

We are both in the habit of reading the morning newspaper. Sometimes we wonder why we waste our time with it, because it seems like every day it's the same old stuff. There's little wisdom there but most of it is just the foolishness of fools made known. A politician seeks another pragmatic solution that causes more problems than it solves. A judge allows a woman to abort her child. A man murders his family, then turns the gun on himself. A businessman deceives his stockholders and employees. The list goes on and on.

But true wisdom rests in the Word of God, and because God has given us that understanding, we try to spend much time there. We want that wisdom to rest in our hearts, to convict us of the sin that remains in us, and to rule over us. True wisdom *is* Christ, who rests in our hearts by faith. Oh, for a closer walk in utter dependence upon His wisdom and grace.

Scriptural Examples

Saul. Although chosen by God to be Israel's king, true wisdom never seemed to rest in Saul's heart. Rather, it was his foolishness that was consistently manifested (1 Sam. 20:30-34).

Nabal. This man made known to all the foolishness that was within him. His wife, Abigail, let her wisdom be known as she treated David and his men with kindness (1 Sam. 25:10-25).

Jesus. Unlimited wisdom rested in the heart of the One who literally *is* the Wisdom of God. His life and His words poured forth the marvelous essence of who He is, as those who walked with Him beheld His glory as that of the only begotten of the Father, full of grace and truth (John 3:34; 1:14; Luke 2:47; John 7:46).

David. After Saul, God anointed David as king in Israel. Unlike Saul, David was a man after the Lord's own heart, and in whose heart rested the wisdom of God (Acts 13:22).

Prayer of Application

Father, You have called me into the rest that is in Christ Jesus. I pray that His wisdom would always rest in my heart, and that I might let His wisdom be made known, even to fools like I once was.

Study Questions and Projects

1) Read Jeremiah 9:23-24. What does the Lord say that we are *not* to glory or boast in? Rather, of what are we to boast? In what things does God, in His wisdom, delight?

2) Read 1 Corinthians 1:18-31. How does Paul describe the wisdom of God for those who are perishing? To those who are being saved? In verse 24, how is Christ described? Do you note a touch of sarcasm in verse 25? Whom do the verses that follow say have been chosen? Why? What three things has Jesus become for us in verse 30? How do these three things show forth the wisdom of God? Discuss with others.

3) How are godly wisdom and its sources described in this list of verses from the Old Testament?

    a) Deuteronomy 29:2-4 - _____

    b) Nehemiah 9:20a - _____

    c) Job 22:21-22 - _____

    d) Job 32:8 - _____

    e) Psalm 25:14 - _____

    f) Proverbs 3:5-6 - _____

    g) Ecclesiastes 2:26 - _____

    h) Isaiah 54:13 - _____

    i) Daniel 1:17 - _____

Other Verses to Study
Matthew 16:16-17; Luke 1:76-79; John 1:1-17; 1 John 2:27.

One to Memorize
A rich man may be wise in his own eyes, but a poor man who has discernment sees through him (Prov. 28:11).

My Personal Action Plan to Be a Woman of Godly Wisdom

1) _____ 2) _____

3) _____ 4) _____

Chapter Twenty

A Woman of Diligence

• •

The woman of wisdom is no sluggard. She "doesn't eat the bread of idleness." But if you'll turn with us to Proverbs 26:13-16, we'll show you a woman who would *feast* on such bread, if she wasn't so doggone lazy. We like to say that this woman is "faithless, feckless, foodless, and foolish."

Notice in 26:13 that she always has an excuse for her inactivity. She won't go outside because she's afraid of her imaginary "lions." She has no faith in God's providence.

Next, like a door stays in the same location, never going anywhere but back and forth, so this feckless woman has no goals or strategies for attaining them. Her life is pointless.

Third, in verse 15, she is foodless. Well, not in the strict sense of the term. She knows the way from the TV to the refrigerator, but she won't feed on God's Word. She might know a few verses—a little milk and baby food—but never chews on the real meat of it.

Finally, she is puffed up by foolish pride, and blind to who she really is. But others see her superficiality as she blusters her way through life. Don't be like her. Instead, follow the diligence of godly wisdom.

Wake Up and Serve the Lord!

Laziness brings on deep sleep, and the shiftless man goes hungry
(Prov. 19:15).

It's no secret that slothfulness can result in poverty. The fate of the college freshman who parties all night should be no mystery to her. She will not be invited back for the second semester. The same is true of the mother who prefers sleep to understanding and filling the needs of her family. Both she and they will go hungry.

But let's apply this proverb to our spiritual lives. Are we just going through the motions in God's service, or is our faith a vibrant, daily reality? Has spiritual sloth cast its deep sleep upon us so that we are barren of fruit? Do we think that laypeople are simply to hire pastors, and then sit back and criticize them? If you are like us, those questions stir your conscience.

We need first the conviction that sloth or laziness in worship, prayer, Bible study, and any service to God is utterly inconsistent with what the Bible teaches. Second, we need to ask God for forgiveness for our shortcomings in this area. What a terrible waste it would be to get to the end of our lives on earth and find out that we were asleep all those years, like Rip Van Winkle.

Scriptural Examples

The Sodomites. God had a lot more against Sodom than sexual sin. They were prideful and arrogant. They ate too much, and they practiced idleness in their apathy (Ezek. 16:49).

The Athenians. They heard Paul speak at the Areopagus. All they did was spend their time doing nothing but talking and listening to the latest ideas. Let's avoid being like the Athenians, and serve the Lord with enthusiasm (Acts 17:21).

Some Thessalonians. Paul had a word for these folks: "busybodies." As Dr. J. Vernon McGee says, "Some people in the church are about as active as termites and with the same result." Paul urged the Thessalonians to diligence (2 Thess. 3:11-13).

Prayer of Application

Father, forgive me for laziness. I know that I have not served You as I ought. Empower me to seek to please You in all things, wanting only Your glory and honor in all that I do.

Practice the Wisdom of Diligence

Lazy hands make a man poor, but diligent hands bring wealth.
He who gathers crops in summer is a wise son, but he who sleeps
during harvest is a disgraceful son (**Prov.** 10:4-5).

These two proverbs display the compound fruits of sloth. On the one hand we see that laziness can make a person poor. Then we also learn that sloth brings disgrace. Sloth therefore becomes not just a material problem, but a moral one as well.

God's commandment to rest on the Sabbath day was well known to the Jews. But the flip side of that commandment instructed them to work six days before they rested (Ex. 23:12). Laziness impoverishes in every way: materially, spiritually, physically, and mentally. It also makes us unprepared for the challenges that lie ahead. Diligence prepares our way, and makes it straight.

The wise son in the verse above labors in preparation for the long winter ahead. Then he and his family will dine on the fruits of his summer's labor. So also, those who are young need to store up knowledge and wisdom in preparation for maturity when the opportunities may be limited. But even when we are older we should never stop learning and growing, applying our minds, hearts, and bodies diligently in all things.

Scriptural Examples

Adam. Adam was given fruitful labor in the Garden of Eden, to tend it and to name its creatures. We're not told how diligent he was in his administration, because he soon became the first man to be fired from his job (Gen 2:15; 19-20).

Joseph. He diligently gathered the crops of Egypt during the time of plenty. When famine came, the wisdom of his diligence became apparent as the storehouses were full (Gen. 41:46-56).

The Athenians. They had nothing to do all day long but sit and listen to the latest gossip. They were the first-century equivalent to today's fans of trashy talk shows (Acts 17:21).

Prayer of Application

Father, help me to be diligent in all things, in whatever role to which You have called me. Your Word says that You love diligence. Help me to walk in it, forsaking all slothfulness.

Don't Be a Sluggard

As vinegar to the teeth and smoke to the eyes, so is a sluggard to those who send him (Prov. 10:26).

There is vivid imagery here. Vinegar will surely set your teeth on edge, and acrid smoke stings and blinds the eyes. A slothful employee is like these distasteful elements.

A central principle of a successful business is to hire good people. Without able employees, one's business is doomed from the start. We who are employers, or who hire employees, need to take this responsibility very seriously.

For those of us who work for an employer, it's important that we do our work diligently, as unto Christ. Even difficult jobs get much easier with Christ by your side, strengthening you and encouraging you. Find the career that utilizes your God-given talents—and one that you enjoy! Then work hard, as well as wisely, and don't be a sluggard.

What are the spiritual implications of this verse? We, too, are "sent"—commissioned by Jesus (Matthew 28:19-20). Are we vinegar to God's teeth and smoke to His eyes? Or are we taking an integral and productive part in the Great Commission for which our Lord has "hired" us? With God's help, let each of us follow Christ's command with diligence, and avoid the path of the sluggard who displeases his boss.

Scriptural Examples

The Laodiceans. Christ addressed one of His seven letters to this church. They were a bunch of "sluggards" whom Jesus promised to "spit out of [His] mouth" (Rev. 3:15-16).

The reluctant son. Jesus told the story of a son who refused to go to work for his dad, but later went. The other son said he'd go, then refused. How this latter young man reminds us of employees who promise so much in the interview, but deliver so little when the chips are down (Matt. 21:28-31).

Prayer of Application

Father, You have called me to be diligent in all things and to do the work to which I am called in a profitable manner. Help me to fulfill that role at my job and in the Great Commission.

Manage Your Resources Prudently

A poor man's field may produce abundant food, but injustice sweeps it away (Prov. 13:23).

This proverb brings to mind the collective farm system of the old Soviet Union that failed to feed the nation. Meanwhile, those who were allowed to plant a small, personal garden had great success. Because of personal incentive and personal responsibility, the individual farmers were able to out-produce the large state farms. In some translations, "injustice" in the last phrase of this proverb is translated "want of judgment." In the Soviet Union, we saw both lack of judgment *and* injustice, and, of course, they are related.

All of us, farmers or not, have resources that we need to manage. Some of us have jobs that require good administrative and supervisory skills. Others work in positions that require great manual skill in the assembly of a product. Still others work at home, managing the affairs of the household. Whatever our occupation, we are given talents that need to be applied and managed if we are to be successful. We are also called to be good stewards of our material possessions, our time, and our study of the Word. In all of these things, God calls us to be wise, just, and diligent.

Scriptural Examples

Joseph. Joseph's tireless administration of Egypt's resources ensured that there would be much food in the time of famine in the land (Gen. 41:33-39).

Solomon. His wise management of Israel saw to it that there was peace and plenty during his reign (1 Kings 4:27-28).

Boaz. He is a fine example of a farmer who managed his people and his harvest with wisdom and prudence. He was well-respected by his employees and took an active role in the farm's administration (Ruth 2:4; 3:2).

Jesus. After feeding the 5,000, Jesus told the disciples to gather up the pieces so that nothing would be wasted (John 6:12).

Prayer of Application

Father, thank You that I am free to grow my own farm, family, business, or career. Give me diligence in management, Lord, and protection from those who would sweep it away unjustly.

Be Diligent in Spiritual Things

The sluggard craves and gets nothing, but the desires of the diligent
are fully satisfied (Prov. 13:4).

We are reminded of the man who approached the piano virtuoso following his concert and said, "I'd give half of my life to play like that." The pianist responded, "Why, that's exactly what I did." The man had the desire, but desire alone wouldn't teach him to play the piano. He needed the diligent study and practice of the concert pianist to reach his aspiration.

Although diligence is profitable in many areas of life, it is indispensible in spiritual things. The Bereans, we're told, didn't just take the things they heard Paul say as the gospel truth. Rather, they searched the Scriptures daily, to see whether or not they were true (Acts 17:11). Don't let anyone tell you that doctrine isn't important. It is only through doctrine that we can have assurance of salvation. We're warned many times in Scripture to beware of false doctrine. (See Matt. 24:11; 24:24; 2 Cor. 11:13; Gal. 2:4.)

But the study of the Scriptures isn't the only way we're to be spiritually diligent. We are to be diligent in prayer (1 Thess. 5:17), in obedience (2 Pet. 3:14), in making our calling sure (2 Pet. 1:10), in guarding against defilement (Heb. 12:15), in every good work (Eph. 2:10), and in instructing our children (Deut. 6:7). God will reward our diligence in seeking to know Him.

Scriptural Examples

Ezra. This man of God returned to Jerusalem to begin reforms among the people. We're told that Ezra was blessed by God as he devoted himself to the study and keeping of God's law, and in teaching it to others (Ezra 7:10).

The Pharisees. These men were commended by Jesus for their diligent study of God's Word. Their problem was that they didn't combine their diligence with faith in Christ, and consequently missed the blessings of that diligence (John 5:39-40).

Prayer of Application

Father, thank You for giving me a desire to follow Your Word in obedience. Help me to make its diligent study and application the top priority in my life, that I may be satisfied.

Let Christ Define Success for You

He who works his land will have abundant food, but he who chases fantasies lacks judgment (**Prov.** 12:11).

This proverb calls the believer to diligence, as does the entire Word of God. While farmers can industriously till, plant, and water their fields, if they fail to follow the Lord's instructions— such as in not allowing their fields a sabbath year (Lev. 25:4)— their diligence will ultimately fail them.

Diligence and industry alone will not provide one with real success. A Christian should seek the Lord's leadership over the "fantasies" of those who define success in worldly ways. We need to recognize that it is God alone who gives us good judgment and all good things, remembering that God calls us to faithfulness (1 Cor. 4:2), and not to the fantasy of worldly "success."

This is particularly true in spiritual matters. What lack of judgment there is in much of the visible church today, as people follow fantasies (2 Pet. 2:3). True believers are exploited while the gospel of Christ is hidden from the unsaved. Beware of those who lack judgment. Instead, be filled with His Word (Ps. 119:11) and diligently till the soil of eternity, satisfied with the abundant food of the Bread of Life (John 6:35). Let Christ define success for you.

Scriptural Examples

Cain. Here is a man who worked his land as a farmer but was void of understanding. He brought some of the fruits of his labor in worship of God, but it was not what God had ordained and was therefore rejected (Gen. 4:2-8).

Uzziah. This king loved agriculture and became very successful as a result. In the end, his power was his undoing. He had not followed God (2 Chron. 26:10-21).

Peter. When Christ confronted him in his fishing boat, he left all and followed his Lord. Peter did not follow fantasies, but let Christ define success for him (2 Pet. 1:16).

Prayer of Application

Father, how often I look to the world to define success. But You are my Creator, and only You have the proper definition. Help me to seek Your will, and not to chase worldly fantasies.

Study Questions and Projects

1) In what areas of life does God require us to be diligent? As you read each of these verses, write down, in your own words, the principle that the Bible teaches. Use another sheet if needed.

    a) Deuteronomy 6:7 - _____

    b) Deuteronomy 6:17 - _____

    c) Deuteronomy 19:18 - _____

    d) 1 Chronicles 22:19 - _____

    e) Proverbs 4:23 - _____

    f) Proverbs 27:23 - _____

    g) Isaiah 55:2 - _____

    h) John 9:4 - _____

    i) 2 Corinthians 8:7 - _____

    j) 1 Timothy 3:10 - _____

    k) 2 Timothy 4:2 - _____

    l) Hebrews 12:15 - _____

    m) 2 Peter 1:5 - _____

    n) 2 Peter 1:10 - _____

    o) 2 Peter 3:14 - _____

2) Read Proverbs 18:9. To whom does Solomon say the sluggard is a brother? Why?

Other Verses to Study
Proverbs 6:6, 9-11; 14:23; 19:15; 19:24 and 20:4; 1 Timothy 5:13.

One to Memorize
Lazy hands make a man poor,
but diligent hands bring wealth (Prov. 10:4).

My Personal Action Plan to Be a Woman of Diligence

1) _____ 2) _____

3) _____ 4) _____

Proverbs 31:28
Her children arise and call her blessed;
her husband also, and he praises her.

Chapter Twenty-One

A Woman Whose Family Is Blessed

●●●●●●●●●●●●●●●●●●●●●●●

What a great joy for a wife and mother to be praised by her family, to be admired and honored because of her wisdom and diligence. Unfortunately, all too often, those who are the most deserving are also the most unappreciated. That's why we didn't entitle this chapter, "A Woman Who Is Praised," because too few are. But that's not the important thing in God's wisdom.

God wants us to bless our families, and it's important to God that we seek our praise from Him alone. By the way, we shouldn't think of "family" in the narrow sense only. Our Christian family is vast and wide-ranging, and is represented principally by our local fellowship of believers. It is important that we are a blessing to that family as well.

The family is a place where we cannot hide. What we are will soon be discovered by all members of it. Perhaps that's why God invented families. To live in such a community where people see you every day without your makeup on, or when you're having a bad day, is tough. If a woman deserves praise after going through all of that, she has pleased God. That's the important thing.

Seek the Lord's Blessing for Your Family

A foolish son is his father's ruin, and a quarrelsome wife is like a constant dripping. Houses and wealth are inherited from parents, but a prudent wife is from the Lord (**Prov. 19:13-14**).

A quarrelling spirit is not the exclusive property of wives. These verses could well be paraphrased, "A foolish daughter is her mother's ruin, and a quarrelsome husband is like a constant dripping. Houses and wealth are inherited from parents, but a prudent husband is from the Lord." Both foolishness and contentiousness destroy trust just as surely as adultery in the marriage and family relationship.

The first phrase of verse 14 only emphasizes the second. While riches may be an inheritance from your father, a prudent wife (or husband) who supports, encourages, and loves his or her spouse, is purely a gift from God.

Without God's rule over a household, life can be miserable. There may be peace for a while, but it is only a matter of time before situations develop that cause strain. Contentions like the continual dripping of a Chinese water torture may commence. If you are single, don't make the mistake of choosing the wrong spouse. Seek godliness in that person above all. Godliness leads to blessings, but contentiousness leads to ruin.

Scriptural Examples

Dinah: a defiled daughter. Her rape by Shechem precipitated the wrath of her brothers, the sons of Jacob. They took revenge on the entire town by tricking all of the men there into being circumcised, and then put them to the sword (Gen. 34).

Peninnah: a quarrelsome wife. Elkanah, the father of Samuel, had two wives, Hannah and this woman. (Perhaps that explains her contentiousness.) Nevertheless, we are told that Peninnah provoked Hannah in order to irritate her. Hannah wept over her taunting (1 Sam. 1:4-8).

Prayer of Application

Dear Lord, thank You for the precious gift of faith. My contentment in You removes all contentiousness. May Your Spirit in me reflect the faithfulness of Christ to others.

Parents and Children, Bless Each Other

Children's children are a crown to the aged, and parents are the pride of their children (Prov. 17:6).

This proverb speaks to what should be, and not to what always is. So often in Scripture, we see the son turning away from the instruction of his righteous parents, or conversely, the parents bringing shame upon their children. Here we see that a woman's grandchildren are a crown to her. What a delight it is to be a grandparent!

God created the family as our first social structure, an institution created for mankind's blessing and well-being. When a man and woman leave their parents and unite to one another (Gen. 2:24), a family is created. If God's will is such, children will come along. Parenthood is a great joy, yet a profound responsibility. But blessing and responsibility are also implied for the children here. They are to honor their parents (Ex. 20:12), who in turn are to raise their children in the nurture and admonition of the Lord (Eph. 6:4). The Christian home should be a great blessing for all who dwell in it.

Scriptural Examples

Adam and Cain. Adam lived to see many generations of his son Cain. God would ultimately destroy them in the Flood. Cain was not a blessing but a curse for Adam. Neither did Cain glory in his father (Gen. 4; Jude 11).

Adam and Seth. God had promised a deliverer to Adam and Eve, and although the first couple may have thought Him to be Cain, it was from the godly line of Seth that He was to come. Adam was surely blessed by Seth's children (Gen. 5).

Timothy. Paul spoke of the excellent witness and faith that lived in Timothy's grandmother, Lois, and his mother, Eunice, and which now lived in him. Surely Timothy was the crowning glory of their lives, as they were of his (2 Tim. 1:5).

Prayer of Application

O, Sovereign Lord, may I be a blessing to my children, raising them with love for You, so that they may one day say that I have been their glory. Lord, that will be glory for You.

Discipline Your Children in the Lord

A foolish son brings grief to his father and bitterness to the one who bore him (Prov. 17:25).

Consistent prayer is needed to change a foolish child into one who wisely seeks after God. But a supplementary medium is also very important. We are to discipline our children daily; to train them in the things of God. If a child grows up to become president of the United States yet is without Christ, that child's parents will surely be full of grief. Prayer is a principle mode of transporting our children into the kingdom, and discipline is the practical part. Without training our prayers are a mockery. But, how do we do it?

It is never too early to start. Read them Bible stories, pray with them, hold regular family devotionals, and involve them in the church where they will be brought into contact with others who share a love for the Lord. Watch over what they are learning at school and at play, and ensure that they get a Christian perspective to offset the world's. Most importantly, be an example to them in your life, that they may see God in and through you.

Scriptural Examples

Cain. Instead of bringing honor to the infant human race, he murdered his brother, Abel, and was sorrowful only about his punishment. Cain was truly a grief to Adam and a bitterness to Eve (Gen. 3:15; 4:1-16).

Esau and his wives. He brought much grief to Isaac and Rebekah. Esau even married Canaanite women specifically to displease his father (Gen. 26:34-35; 28:8-9).

Absalom. In Absalom's treachery, he brought great grief to David, particularly in his own foolish death (2 Sam. 18:33).

Timothy. Here again is this son who was a joy, and not a bitterness, to her that bore him. His mother, Eunice, evidently trained Timothy from infancy in the Holy Scriptures, and the result was the sincere faith of a man of God (2 Tim. 1:5; 3:15).

Prayer of Application

Lord, give me discernment in bringing up my children. May I always discipline them in the context of loving patience, remembering that my ultimate desire is for their salvation.

Mothers, Teach Your Children the Right Path

The sayings of King Lemuel—an oracle his mother taught him: "O my son, O son of my womb, O son of my vows, do not spend your strength on women, your vigor on those who ruin kings. It is not for kings, O Lemuel—not for kings to drink wine, not for rulers to crave beer, lest they drink and forget what the law decrees, and deprive all the oppressed of their rights. Give beer to those who are perishing, wine to those who are in anguish; let them drink and forget their poverty and remember their misery no more. Speak up for those who cannot speak for themselves, for the rights of all who are destitute. Speak up and judge fairly; defend the rights of the poor and needy" (Prov. 31:1-9).

There never was a king of Israel named Lemuel, so this is perhaps a nickname given to Solomon by his mother, Bathsheba. *Lemuel* literally means *under God* or *with God*. Bathsheba treasured her son, particularly after the loss of her first child (2 Sam. 12:19). Perhaps she taught him this oracle, trusting that he would be king one day. If so, he would need protection against three opponents: "wine, women, and song."

She knew firsthand of David's affinity for the opposite sex. Here she joins God in warning against a multiplicity of wives (Deut. 17:17). Eventually, Solomon would take 700 wives and 300 concubines (1 Kings 11:1-3).

Next, she warned her boy about the damaging effects that alcoholic beverages can have. Kings don't need to be anesthetized, they need to bring proper justice and wisdom to their subjects.

Finally, Bathsheba warned him against frivolity and favoritism. Instead, he should take up the song of the poor and destitute, and not just the song of the established and affluent. Solomon did reign in justice and treated the poor with dignity.

Mothers, your sons and daughters need oracles from you, too. What greater legacy than to be a guide to the right pathway?

Prayer of Application

Father, thank You for mothers who provide godly guidance to their children. May this oracle provide an outline for modern day moms wishing to see their kids walk with You.

Bring Joy to Your Mother and Father

*A wise son brings joy to his father, but a foolish son
grief to his mother* (Prov. 10:1).

There is a sense in which the Bible is a record book of wise and foolish sons and daughters who either blessed or cursed their parents. On page after page we find examples of men and women who brought either joy or grief to their moms and dads.

Adam, the son of God, grieved his Father. Adam was in turn grieved heavily by Cain, but blessed by both Abel and Seth. The patriarch Abraham was blessed by Isaac, who in turn was grieved by Jacob. The list goes on.

Notice it is the wise son who brings joy and the foolish son who brings grief. Proverbs 1:7 and 9:10 say that wisdom begins with the fear of the Lord. All wisdom flows from that spring. The foolish son, on the other hand, despises the Lord and His instruction. And so it is in our relationship to the Lord that we bring our parents joy. Someone may say, "My parents couldn't care less about God. They are upset about my faith in Christ. Have I failed to honor them?" No. You owe more allegiance to your Father in heaven. To bring Him joy is your greater calling.

Scriptural Examples

Noah. Lamech named his son Noah—"comfort"—because Noah would comfort his parents in the labor of the soil that God had cursed. Noah did prove to be a wise son who feared the Lord, preached of His righteousness, and followed His instructions to the letter (Gen. 5:28-29; 2 Pet. 2:5; Heb. 11:7).

Ham, Shem, and Japheth. These sons of Noah are the ancestors of all who walk the earth. Following the Flood, Noah foolishly got drunk and lay naked in his tent. Ham disgraced his father by looking at his nakedness and telling his brothers about it. But Shem and Japheth backed into the tent and covered their father, thereby honoring him (Gen. 9:21-23).

Prayer of Application

Dear God, comfort and strengthen parents who must suffer in the wake of a son or daughter who runs from You. At the same time, help us children to honor our parents out of love for You.

Leave the Inheritance of a Godly Life

A good man leaves an inheritance for his children's children, but a sinner's wealth is stored up for the righteous (Prov. 13:22).

One glance at this proverb will reveal that it couldn't affect all of us. Some aren't blessed with children or grandchildren. Good people may die penniless. And do we see sinners' wealth given to the just? We must look beyond the material to the spiritual to see the truth of the proverb.

The godly woman, regardless of the children in her life, leaves an inheritance to future generations. The inheritance is her holy example, her godly walk in the reverence of her Lord, and her intercessory prayer that has yet to be answered. The prayers of a righteous woman have a far-reaching effect.

The wealth of the sinner stored up for the just is a common occurrence in the Old Testament. For example, we see Laban's going to Jacob (Gen. 31:1-16); Egypt's to Israel (Ex. 12:35-36); and Haman's to Esther and Mordecai (Est. 8:1-2). What wealth will today's sinner leave for the just? It will be most likely the earth, which the meek will inherit when their Lord returns (Matt. 5:5).

Scriptural Examples

Abraham. God's covenant to Abraham was to be inherited by all generations. It was based on Abraham's faith in God's words. What a blessing this inheritance from a good man is for us today, as we are heirs of the promise that was given to him so many years ago (Gen. 15; 17:7).

Caleb. The righteous Caleb received Hebron as his inheritance from the Lord. This land was passed on from generation to generation of this fine man's descendants (Josh. 14:14).

The Egyptians. As Israel was preparing to flee Egypt, Moses instructed the people to ask the Egyptians for silver and gold. God opened the hearts of the Egyptian people, and they gave the Israelites great treasure (Ex. 12:35-36).

Prayer of Application

Dear Lord and God, thank You for the inheritance You have given me in Christ Jesus. Lead me in a life that is pleasing to You, that my children and their children will be blessed by it.

Study Questions and Projects

1) Read the following proverbs and give a short reason why the woman's family was *not* blessed by her.

     a.) Proverbs 14:1 - _____

     b.) Proverbs 19:13b - _____

     c.) Proverbs 21:9 - _____

     d.) Proverbs 21:19 - _____

     e.) Proverbs 27:15 - _____

     f.) Proverbs 30:23 - _____

2) In Genesis 2:24, we are given a foundational verse for God's establishment of the family unit. What is the man to do as concerns his relationship with his father and mother? Do you think that applies to the woman as well? What does it mean to "leave" your father and mother? Have you seen a marriage that was not blessed because this principle wasn't followed? Discuss with others.

3) What advice does Paul give to the older women in Titus 2:3-5? In what way are they to train the younger women? What reason does he give? Do you have a relationship with a younger or older woman, in which you are encouraging each other in these things?

4) What do Proverbs 29:15 and 17 tell us about correcting our children? What will be the fruit of such correction?

Other Verses to Study
Deuteronomy 6:7; 11:18-21; 32:46; Proverbs 22:6, 15; 23:13-14.

One to Memorize
Children's children are a crown to the aged,
and parents are the pride of their children (Prov.17:6).

My Personal Action Plan to Be a Woman Whose Family Is Blessed

1) _____ 2) _____

3) _____ 4) _____

- Proverbs 31:29 -
*"Many women do noble things,
but you surpass them all."*

Chapter Twenty-Two

A Woman of Integrity
•••••••••••••••••••••••••••

Bob has a prayer that speaks well to this topic taped into an old Bible:

> O God, help me to live what I say I believe
> so that others in me may see,
> The fruit of the Spirit that Christ alone
> could ever produce in me.
>
> Help me to live what I say I believe
> as I begin each bright new day,
> So that those around me will want to know
> the Person who makes me that way.
>
> Help me to live what I say I believe
> So my children will know it's true;
> That Christ is real and ready to help
> with everything they must do.
>
> Yes, Lord, help me to live what I say I believe—
> true, it's an enormous task.
> But praise be to God that He's promised His help,
> and all I need do is . . . ask!

Anonymous

To *live* what we *say* we believe is the essence of integrity. The woman of Proverbs 31 surpassed in her deeds "many women who do noble things." She didn't just talk the walk; she walked it. Our prayer is that these proverbs will guide you along that same path.

Walk the Straight Path of Integrity

The man of integrity walks securely, but he who takes crooked paths will be found out (Prov. 10:9).

The dictionary defines integrity as "soundness of moral character; a sound, unimpaired condition, or wholeness and completeness." A woman of integrity is one who has adopted certain moral principles in life, and then walks according to them. For the woman of God, the Bible forms the basis of those principles. The Bible is the Christian's *only* authority for faith and life. Only the Bible can bind her conscience. Therefore, if the Christian is to walk in integrity, she must walk in conformity to God's Word. To do so is to walk securely, without fear of failure or shame. All other ways are crooked.

How do we obey this proverb's principle and keep on the path of integrity? The bad news is that we can't. However, the good news is that the Spirit of God working in our hearts by faith can! We can do all things through Him (Phil. 4:13).

Scriptural Examples

Enoch and the antidiluvians. Enoch walked so closely in integrity with his God that God took him home. He never tasted death. All the while, he lived among people who walked in crooked paths (Gen. 5:22-24; 6:5; Heb. 11:5).

Hanani. Nehemiah put this man in charge of Jerusalem because he was a man of integrity who feared God (Neh. 7:2).

Job. God commended Job as a man who feared God and walked in integrity. Job would be the first to tell us that his integrity came only from his God (Job 1:8; 2:3; 2:9; 6:29; 27:5).

Ananias and Sapphira. This couple was on a crooked path. God took them home, but not like Enoch (Acts 5:1-10).

Peter. Peter was one who got off the path. Paul found out and rebuked Peter because he had left the true gospel in order to appease the Judaizers (Gal. 2:11-14).

Prayer of Application

Sovereign Lord, thank You for Your Word and for the Holy Spirit who helps me to follow its secure path. May I always walk in its light, to the end that You will be glorified in me.

If You Vow, Be Sure to Follow Through

It is a trap for a man to dedicate something rashly and only later to consider his vows (**Prov. 20:25**).

There is a saying in wartime that "there are no atheists in foxholes." Faced with the imminent prospect of death, many have made rash promises to God. The problem is not the voluntary promise or vow. The problem comes when one fails to follow through. We sin when we promise—to God or to others—without first counting the cost.

Solomon writes that it is better to keep your mouth shut than to make a vow that you don't keep (Eccl. 5:4-5). Some, caught up in religious fervor, will make a rash vow to God without considering the cost (2 Pet. 2:21-22). We have both volunteered to do things that have become a burden as we struggled to follow through. Better to say "No" than to say "Yes" and then back out.

God is very serious about promises. He will deliver on every detail of every promise He has ever made, and He expects no less of us. What a joy it is for the Christian to understand that He does so. But what an awesome responsibility it is to follow in His footsteps.

Scriptural Examples

Jepthah. Israel's judge made a rash vow that if God would grant him victory, whatever would come out of his house first upon his return home he would sacrifice as a burnt offering. It was his daughter, his only child (Judg. 11:29-40).

The Israelites. The Benjamites were slaughtered by the other tribes. Then they vowed not to allow their daughters to marry Benjamites. The tribe almost perished (Judg. 20–21).

Hannah. She made a vow to God that if He would give her a son she would dedicate him to His service. God granted her request, and as soon as the boy Samuel was weaned, she took him to Eli. Hannah followed through on her vows (1 Sam. 1:11-24).

Prayer of Application

Precious Savior, thank You for following through on the promise that a sacrifice would be provided for my sins. Help me, in like manner, to follow through on the promises I make.

Avoid Hypocrisy at All Costs

"It's no good, it's no good!" says the buyer; then off he goes and
boasts about his purchase (**Prov. 20:14**).

The hypocrite is deceitful. She says one thing with her lips, but
her heart is in another place. Here we see a buyer who bad-mouths
the seller's product, hoping to strike a better deal. So what he
knows is good he says is bad. The seller, on the other hand, might
attempt to deceive the buyer by claiming some benefit of his
product that it cannot deliver. For the Christian application, we
may talk the talk of faith, but fail to walk the walk. This is
hypocrisy.

We live in a world of inconsistency. We are promised something verbally, but on reading the fine print we find the opposite
is true. Advertisements promise enjoyment for smokers, but
cigarettes deliver cancer, emphysema, and heart disease. Fashion
models promise the glamour and sex appeal of a "perfect" body,
but deliver anorexia and bulimia to their disillusioned fans. The
world offers fulfillment and satisfaction in so many ways but in
the end delivers guilt and shame. Only in Christ can we find the
consistency that brings full joy and peace and confidence. Follow
Him and avoid the trap of the world's hypocrisy.

Scriptural Examples

The Israelites. Time and again they would honor God with
their lips, yet their hearts and minds were unfaithful to His
covenant with them (Ps. 78:34-38).

The adulteress. She promised the simple-minded youth enjoyment in her bed. It was safe. Her husband was on a long trip.
The youth followed her, little knowing that while she promised
sweetness and excitement, she delivered death (Prov. 7:10-23).

The Pharisees. Jesus called them hypocrites (Matt. 15:7), and
warned his disciples of their devious ways. They were false prophets who kept men from the kingdom (Luke 11:39-52).

Prayer of Application

Father in heaven, keep my life free from hypocrisy. As I grow
in Christ, help me to follow His commands consistently, that my
life will bear the fruit of that which my lips speak.

Beware the Consequences of the Selfish Lie

A false witness will not go unpunished, and he who pours out lies will not go free. A false witness will not go unpunished, and he who pours out lies will perish (**Prov. 19:5, 9**).

Deceit is a common theme in Proverbs. Notice that in verse 5 the liar "will not go free," while in verse 9, we see his final forecast of doom. The truth is a fragile thing, and easily bent or broken. Shading the truth ever so slightly where the listener is deceived is a gross offense before God.

But what about times when lying actually preserves lives, such as those who protected Jews hiding from the Nazis before and during World War II? Is it always wrong to lie? Scripture itself has several instances where lies have been utilized for good and not for evil. We are reminded of the Egyptian midwives who lied to Pharaoh (Ex. 1:15-19). There was also Ehud, who presented tribute before Eglon, the Moabite king, before dispatching him with a double-edged sword (Judg. 3:16-21).

The answer, we believe, is in the motivation for the deed. If our motive is injustice, greed, convenience, or to elevate self, then lying is always wrong.

Scriptural Examples

Pharaoh. Time after time Pharaoh lied when he promised to let God's people go. Only after the death of all of the firstborn did Pharaoh let the people go. But he was not to escape God's wrath. He went swimming in the Red Sea (Ex. 7-14).

The disobedient son. Jesus told this short parable. A man asked both his sons to work in his vineyard. One said "No," but then he later went to work. The second said that he would go, but never did. Which of the two did his father's will? The first. The second was a liar and a deserter (Matt. 21:23-31).

Rahab. She lied to the elders of her city and saved Israel's spies. Her name was eternally written in God's hall of fame (Heb. 11:31).

Prayer of Application

Sovereign Lord, keep my tongue from lies. Sometimes I am tempted to shade the truth just a little for a selfish motive. Strengthen me, Lord, that I tell the truth in all such instances.

Do Not Manipulate Others

If a ruler listens to lies, all his officials become wicked
(Prov. 29:12).

The sinful underlings of a ruler have a tendency to change into whatever the ruler wants them to be. If he wants to hear lies, they will tell him what he wants to hear. If he wants to be flattered, they will flatter him. They will do whatever is necessary to shore up their position in his court. They will try to manipulate him to control the situation.

Were you ever on a date and sensed that you were being manipulated? Perhaps the fellow called but then was not in touch for weeks. You may have sensed that he tried to control every situation by his mood changes. Bob once had a high-ranking employee who would *say* in meetings whatever he thought Bob wanted to hear. Then, when he went back to his desk, he would *do* just the opposite. Eventually, Bob had to fire him—he was manipulative.

Be yourself! Treat your boss, your spouse, your friends, your employees, and everyone else in the same way: openly and honestly. Be transparent. Don't be a chameleon who changes to fit every situation in order to deceive and manipulate others.

Scriptural Examples

Jehoshaphat, Ahab and his prophets, and Micaiah. Judah and Israel joined forces to make war on Aram. Ahab summoned 400 prophets who told him the lie he wanted to hear. But Jehoshaphat insisted on a prophet of the Lord. Ahab reluctantly sent for Micaiah, who was no chameleon. He spoke openly and honestly before the kings, predicting failure (1 Kings 22:6-28).

Shadrach, Meshach, and Abednego. Nebuchadnezzar ordered all in his kingdom to fall down and worship the image he had made of himself. These three refused, openly declaring their allegiance to God. They were thrown into the fiery furnace for refusing to perjure themselves to please the king (Dan. 3:1-20).

Prayer of Application

Jesus, You never change. You're the same yesterday, today and forever. May I never alter my behavior to manipulate or control situations or people. Help me to trust You for all of life's outcomes.

Practice Spirit-Control and Honesty

*A quick-tempered man does foolish things, and
a crafty man is hated* (**Prov. 14:17**).

Many women, in their misconception that the events of this
world are not subject to the government of God, react angrily in
situations that do not please them. In doing so, they prove their
foolishness. Further, some women plan wicked or crafty schemes
to cheat others, not understanding that the Lord knows their every
thought.

The spiritual woman should understand that the Lord is
working all events and circumstances out for His glory, and for the
ultimate good of His own (Rom. 8:28-29). The world view of the
spiritual woman provides no room for hasty anger, even though
sometimes events seem to warrant it. When we feel provoked, we
are to prayerfully seek the control of the Spirit.

The woman of God will not be crafty or dishonest. She is aware
of the omniscience and holiness of her Lord. This should be self-
evident, but we should understand that it applies to every detail of
life. The Christian should always seek to conduct herself in the
reverence and awe of a Holy God.

Scriptural Examples

Balaam. This false prophet's donkey saw the angel of the Lord
and lay down on the trail. Balaam, in anger, beat the donkey. His
eyes were then opened, and he, too, saw the angel (Num. 22:27-31).

Asa. Hanani, a seer, came to this king of Judah and condemned
him for trusting in other men, rather than in the Lord God. Asa
was enraged and had Hanani thrown into prison. The king
continued to oppress his subjects (2 Chron. 16:10).

Jesus. When falsely accused and beaten at His trial before
Pilate, He stood in silence. If the Creator of the universe can
maintain such self-control, how can we mere creatures do otherwise? (Matt. 27:12-14).

Prayer of Application

Dear Lord, by Your Spirit working in me, help me to control
my anger in situations where I am tempted to strike out at others.
Help me also to speak the truth even when it hurts.

Study Questions and Projects

1) Moses' father-in-law, Jethro, visited him in the wilderness and advised Moses to select men to help him in the administration of the people. Exodus 18:21 gives Jethro's recommendations for the qualities of character these men should possess. What are they? Do you agree with his list? Are there any qualities you would add?

2) What commandment does God give in Deuteronomy 16:19-20 that has bearing on integrity? How does God's command here reflect Jethro's thinking?

3) Job was a man of consummate integrity. (See God's view of Job's integrity in Job 2:3.) In chapter 31, Job lists some of those aspects of his life that reflected what he believed in his heart. See how many you can find and write them on a piece of paper. How many of the subjects that he discusses bear direct relationship to one of the Ten Commandments? Finally, look for overarching reasons Job gives for living this way. Discuss with others.

4) In Philippians 4:8, Paul gives us a list of topics to think on. Can you list them all? _____, _____, _____,

_____, _____, _____, _____

or _____. Why is God concerned with our thoughts? What admonition does Paul add in verse 9?

Other Verses to Study
Matthew 15:1-20; Colossians 3:22-23; 1 Peter 2:12; 3:16.

One to Memorize
The man of integrity walks securely, but he who takes crooked paths will be found out (Prov. 10:9).

My Personal Action Plan to Be a Woman of Integrity

1) _____ 2) _____

3) _____ 4) _____

- Proverbs 31:30 -
Charm is deceptive, and beauty is fleeting;
but a woman who fears the Lord is to be praised.

Chapter Twenty-Three

A Woman Who
Fears the Lord
• • • • • • • • • • • • • • • • • • •

Think back again to your days in high school. Remember the most popular kids? They probably had one or both of the "fleeting"qualities mentioned above. They either had great, outgoing personalities ("charm"), or they were exceptionally good-looking ("beauty"). Some had both. Those qualities were very important in high school, but looking back they seem superficial. We have found that other things like honesty, kindness, moral strength, diligence, justice, and so forth are much more important for a person to have. In this view of the wisdom woman we see the *most* important characteristic she can have: to "fear the Lord."

In this set of proverbs we will look at what it means to fear the Lord and how such fear works itself out in our lives. Bob developed an acronym to help remember what it is to fear the Lord: F-E-A-R. "F" stands for Facts. We first need to know whom it is we fear. We want to *know* Christ. "E" is for Enjoyment. We are called to find our joy in God and to glorify Him only. "A" is for Active Obedience. We don't obey God because we *have* to. We obey Him because we *want* to. Finally, "R" stands for Reverential Awe. Our God is the God of fearsome majesty. That is exactly why we can enjoy Him. He loves us and He is in absolute control.

191

Fear the Lord

The fear of the Lord is the beginning of knowledge, but fools despise wisdom and discipline (**Prov. 1:7**).

Proverbs is all about godly decision-making. In this verse we come face-to-face with our first decision: what shall we do with God? If one doesn't get this decision right, all of the decisions that follow in her life will be wrong as well.

As a woman studies the Bible she begins to see something startling about our Creator. There is no middle ground with God. On the one hand, He is a God of ultimate wrath, and on the other, a God of ultimate love. Our God is altogether righteous and holy, and He demands the same of us, His creatures.

What does it mean to "fear the Lord"? That day when He opened our eyes and we first beheld His holiness over our sinfulness, we shivered at the realization that there was nothing we could do to avoid His wrath. Then, when we understood that God Himself had provided the solution in Jesus Christ, and that He lovingly held out His salvation to us as a free gift, our trembling fear turned to an affectionate reverence and awe.

Many who are in pews today are practical atheists. They don't tremble before God, and neither do they hold Him in affectionate awe. They are the fools of whom this proverb speaks. Don't walk with them. Fear the Lord, and be obedient to His every commandment. That fear is the beginning of wisdom's path.

Scriptural Examples

Korah. This Levite and his followers despised the leadership of Moses and Aaron. In their insolence, they showed their lack of fear of God. God opened the earth and swallowed Korah, as his followers faced fire from heaven (Num. 16:1-34).

Judas. There has never been a greater fool than Judas. He walked with the Lord throughout His earthly ministry, yet despised His wisdom and discipline (Matt. 27:3-5).

Prayer of Application

Dear God, thank You for Your Word that makes us tremble at Your power and wrath. But thank you most of all for Your Son who gives us His righteousness. May I follow Him always.

Fear God and Depart from Evil

*A wise man fears the Lord and shuns evil, but a fool is
hotheaded and reckless* (Prov. 14:16).

The non-Christian woman either denies the existence of God,
or she fashions God in her own image. Her God perhaps wound
things up eons ago, and sat down in His big easy chair to watch
history unfold. This woman confidently goes her own self-willed
way, often hotheaded and reckless because she has no ultimate
authority on whom to call nor who will call her to account.

The spiritual woman, on the other hand, has an understanding
of the sovereignty of her God. She knows that He is working all of
her circumstances toward the accomplishment of His purposes
and for His glory (Phil. 2:12-13). God is in absolute, moment-by-
moment control of His creation. He has granted people free will
that will ultimately be confronted with judgment (Acts 17:31). So,
the spiritual woman flees from evil, knowing the holiness of the
Lord (2 Cor. 5:11). The wisdom woman knows that all sin is vanity
anyway, and will bring ultimate disappointment (Rom. 6:21).

Scriptural Examples

Rehoboam. Solomon's reckless son had confidence in the
foolish advice of his young friends. He plunged into a course that
would lead ultimately to his own destruction and to the division
of Judah and Israel (1 Kings 12:13-15).

Sennacherib. This self-confident Assyrian monarch mocked
the name of the Lord. In response to Sennacherib's insults and
foolish provocation, God sent His angel through the Assyrian
camp and destroyed 185,000 soldiers (2 Kings 19:28-37).

Zacchaeus. This wealthy tax collector had cheated many of the
citizens of Jericho. But on his encounter with Jesus, the fear of the
Lord came into his heart. He repented and offered to give half of
his possessions to the poor and to pay back those he had cheated
by four times the amount he had stolen (Luke 19:1-10).

Prayer of Application

Father, show me the sin that remains in my life and give me the
strength to avoid even the slightest deviation from Your holy way.
May I warn others of the foolishness of sin against You.

Live Out the Gospel of Christ

Through love and faithfulness sin is atoned for; through the fear of the Lord a man avoids evil (Prov. 16:6).

Mankind's "love and faithfulness," or "mercy and truth" (as the KJV translates the phrase), don't amount to a hill of beans when it comes to eternal life. Only through God's mercy and truth, the God-man Jesus Christ, can our iniquity be purged, our sin atoned for. Mankind seeks to expunge sin through outward ceremonies and doing good works, but God does it with the once and for all sacrifice of His Son, applied by the Holy Spirit (Heb. 7:27).

Does the woman whose debt to the law of God is paid continue to habitually practice sin? God forbid! (Rom. 6:2) The new birth places in us a reverential fear of God and a hatred of sin, so that the child of God *must* depart from evil. Will she therefore become perfect and never sin again? No. As long as she is in this earthly body, there is always occasion to sin, but not the habit of it. Sin will be crowded out by a desire to live for God.

What, then, ought we to do, knowing that the gospel of Christ is our only hope? We need to follow Christ's command to *give out* the gospel to our neighbors (Matt. 28:19), and most importantly, to *live out* the gospel each day of our lives.

Scriptural Examples

David. David cried out to God to purge his iniquity. He saw himself as a sinner since his conception. Only the mercy and truth of God could cleanse him. Cleansed, he desired to depart from evil and teach others the fear of the Lord (Ps. 51:5-13).

Paul. Paul said that he had kept the law of God perfectly, and yet he later counted all his law-keeping as garbage (Phil. 3:6-8). On the road to Damascus, an alien righteousness was given to him (Phil. 3:9), and he began to live a life of faith, not of works. He began giving out the gospel of Christ, and personally pressed on to the prize of the high calling of Christ Jesus (Phil. 3:13-14).

Prayer of Application

Sovereign Lord, how I thank You for saving me through Christ. Give me strength and courage that I might tell others of Your love. May Your glory be known throughout the world.

Thrive on the Law of the Lord

Blessed is the man who always fears the Lord, but he who hardens his heart falls into trouble (**Prov. 28:14**).

What does it mean to "fear the Lord" on a consistent basis? It begins with an understanding of the gospel: of who we are and who God is, and the great gulf between us that has been bridged by Jesus Christ. It means to live in utter dependence upon His providence and to trust His Word to guide us. It means to love His law and to obey it (Ps. 119:97, 113, 163 and 165).

We who have been born again have no need to fear the Lord's condemnation (Rom. 8:1). We are given a desire to serve and please Him who brings us liberty. No longer is God's law understood to be a taskmaster that we must keep perfectly in order to be saved. The law never saved anyone (Rom. 3:20). Rather, the law has become an expression of God's grace, and we should love it.

The person who fears the Lord wants to keep the moral law for two basic reasons. First, she stands in awe of her God and she wants to please Him. Second, she realizes that God, in His infinite wisdom, has given us His law as a guide to a happy, fulfilling, and productive life. The Christian puts God's wisdom above her own, and relies completely upon God's judgment.

Hardness of heart is simply unbelief (Heb. 3:15-19). Those who turn their backs on God's way fall into trouble, just as the Israelites, who refused to trust and believe God in the wilderness. Don't be like them. Fear the Lord and thrive on every word that proceeds from His mouth (Deut. 8:3).

Scriptural Examples

Shadrach, Meschach, and Abednego. These fine men feared the Lord much more than they feared the Babylonian king's flames. They were blessed of God as they survived the oven without so much as a singed beard. But they declared that even if they died in the fire, they wouldn't forsake their God (Dan. 3:16-18).

Prayer of Application

Father, thank You for Your law, which provides a lamp for my eyes and a path for my feet, keeping me from sin and trouble. May my feet never stumble into pathways of unbelief.

Find Wisdom's Healthy Body

Do not be wise in your own eyes; fear the Lord and shun evil. This
will bring health to your body and nourishment to your bones
(**Prov. 3:7-8**).

We've all known someone who was "a legend in her own mind"—wise in her own eyes. But we are commanded to "fear the Lord and shun evil." These are opposite sides of the same coin. If we honor the Lord, we will hate sin (Prov. 8:3). When we turn to Christ for salvation, we turn away from sin (Prov.14:27; Rom. 12:9). Christ and sin are like oil and water; they don't mix.

God's love for us always seeks what is best for us. Sin does not. There are many temporal consequences of sin. For instance, drunkenness produces cirrhosis, cancer, car crashes, divorce, spousal abuse and the like.

California abounds with health clubs where people seek bodily fitness. There are some wonderful spas where one can exercise and get massages, facials, herbal wraps—the works. Now all this is fine, but we belong to a different kind of health club. It's called a "church." Within our "health club" we learn to fear the Lord and to live according to His commandments. As the wisdom woman of Proverbs 31 knew, "Charm is deceptive, and beauty is fleeting; but a woman who fears the Lord is to be praised."

Scriptural Examples

Gehazi. After Elisha's healing of Naaman, the prophet's servant ran after the visitor, seeking the payment that Elisha had refused. Because of his sin, Gehazi was stricken with the same leprosy from which Naaman had been healed. Gehazi did not "fear the Lord and shun evil" (2 Kings 5).

Uzziah. This king of Judah had feared the Lord, but became prideful in his latter years and sinned when he burned incense in the temple. God sent upon Uzziah the same leprosy that Gehazi had received, but it never healed (2 Chron. 26:5; 16-23).

Prayer of Application

Father, help me to meet You each day in reverence and awe, and to follow Your leadership in all things, not allowing sin a foothold in my life. Surely it will mean health and peace for me.

Fear the One Who Gives Life

The fear of the Lord adds length to life, but the years of the wicked are cut short (Prov. 10:27).

There are perhaps three senses in which the fear of the Lord brings "long life." First, our actual number of days on this earth may be lengthened by a life led by the Holy Spirit. Our habits will be purer, and our minds will not be beset with worry and anxiety. Second, the days themselves will be longer, as we are given a fuller, more meaningful life by our Savior (John 10:10). The third sense, of course, is that our years will never end if we continue in the fear of the Lord (Heb. 6:11-12).

The wicked woman's years are cut short. Her worldliness and bad health habits may do it. Even if she should live many years, they will be years filled with the guilt and sorrow that accompany unforgiven sin. She will never know the new life that God provides by grace, choosing instead to cling to her worthless idols (Jonah 2:8). When the unsaved woman dies, her death, unlike that of the Christian, is an eternal death, not an eternal life.

Scriptural Examples

Jehoram. This wicked king's life was cut short at age 40, but more importantly we're told that his death brought no one's regret. He wasn't even given the honor of being buried in the tombs of the kings of Israel. He, like many other kings of Israel, failed to fear the One who could bring life (2 Chron. 21:6, 20).

Judas. His days were cut short as he threw himself over the precipice of suicide into an eternity of darkness. He walked the dusty trails of Judea with the One who gives life, yet he chose instead the way of death (Matt 27:1-10).

Jesus. Weren't his days "cut short"? Yes, but only because He took upon Himself our wickedness, and died in our place upon the cross, to the end that we might have life. His years were cut short for us (Isa. 53:4-6; Heb. 1:8).

Prayer of Application

Eternal God, thank You for the new life that You have given me by grace alone. I deserved death, but in Your infinite mercy, You resurrected me to a new and living hope. Thank You, Jesus.

Study Questions and Projects

1) It might surprise some to think of the "enjoyment of the Lord" as a part of "fear of the Lord." Look up the following verses in the Psalms and write down, in your own words, the ways that the psalmists say we are to get enjoyment from knowing God.

    a) Psalm 2:11 - _____

    b) Psalm 5:11 - _____

    c) Psalm 13:5 - _____

    d) Psalm 16:11 - _____

    e) Psalm 19:8 - _____

    f) Psalm 28:7 - _____

    g) Psalm 42:4 - _____

    h) Psalm 63:7 - _____

    i) Psalm 85:6 - _____

    j) Psalm 97:11 - _____

    k) Psalm 119:162 - _____

    l) Psalm 126:5-6 - _____

    m) Psalm 149:2 - _____

2) In John 15:8, Jesus says, "This is to my Father's glory, that you bear much fruit." What is the fruit of fearing God as listed in Galatians 5:22-23?

Other Verses to Study

Joshua 24:14; 2 Corinthians 5:10-11; 1 Peter 2:17.

One to Memorize

Do not be wise in your own eyes; fear the Lord and shun evil. This will bring health to your body and nourishment to your bones (Prov. 3:7-8).

My Personal Action Plan to Be a Woman Who Fears the Lord

1) _____ 2) _____

3) _____ 4) _____

- **Proverbs 31:31-**
Give her the reward she has earned,
and let her works bring her praise at the city gate.

Chapter Twenty-Four

A Woman Who Is Rewarded
• • • • • • • • • • • • • • • • • •

Perhaps the first thing to notice about this last verse describing our wonderful woman of wisdom is that she has been praised by her family (vs. 28), for her fear of the Lord (vs. 30), and now by all the people of the community. But is that all of the reward she has earned—the praise of others for the works she has done? On the other hand, is salvation her reward? That can't be! The Bible is clear that we are saved by God's grace, through faith, and not by our works (Gen. 15:6; Rom. 3:21-22; 8:1-4; Eph. 2:8-9).

But Paul tells us that we must all appear before the judgment seat of Christ (Rom. 14:10; 2 Cor. 5:10). Judgment presupposes penalties and rewards. Otherwise, God's commandments would be negotiable. But ours will not be a judgment unto condemnation or salvation (Rom. 8:1; 1 Cor. 3:12-15); rather, it will be a judgment unto rewards. It is by God's grace that the wisdom woman will receive eternal rewards in heaven for her earthly good works.

Jesus commands His followers to "store up for yourselves treasures in heaven" (Matt. 6:19-21). Christians are to have the long view; to work by faith for treasures that do not perish, but which we must die to obtain. The short view wants all its rewards in this life. We think the wisdom woman had that long view of life.

Prepare for the Judgment Seat of Christ

If you falter in times of trouble, how small is your strength! Rescue those being led away to death; hold back those staggering toward slaughter. If you say "But we knew nothing about this," does not he who weighs the heart perceive it? Does not he who guards your life know it? Will he not repay to each person according to what he has done? (Prov. 24:10-12).

Many people think that they will not be held accountable for what they do. But Paul says, "For we must all appear before the judgment seat of Christ, that each one may receive what is due him for the things done while in the body, whether good or bad. Since, then, we know what it is to fear the Lord, we try to persuade men" (2 Cor. 5: 8-11; Rom. 14:10-12). There will be a judgment day for believers: not unto condemnation, (Rom. 8:1), but unto rewards. Believers who have laid up "treasures in heaven" (Matt. 6:19-20) will be rewarded, while others will suffer loss (1 Cor. 3:12-15).

These verses portray an omniscient Judge who sees through our excuses. When we get out of our comfort zone (vs. 10a), we may shrink back. We say, "That's not my responsibility," or "I'm not gifted in that." We may follow only those commandments we find enjoyable. We may plead ignorance (vs. 12a), but that's a flimsy excuse that God sees through.

Paul says, "Wait until the Lord comes. He will bring to light what is hidden in darkness and expose the motives of men's hearts" (1 Cor. 4:5). Who is He that "guards your life" (vs. 12b) but this same Lord? He will give us strength to overcome fear (2 Cor. 12:9).

Scriptural Examples

Faith's hall of fame. Hebrews 11 gives a glowing record of men and women of faith. Note particularly Moses, who looked forward to his reward, and also those saints who refused to be released from torture to obtain a better resurrection. Surely they were all prepared for Christ's judgment seat.

Prayer of Application

Heavenly Father, Your grace is overwhelming. We not only are given heaven, but treasures beyond imagining. Help me to desire a better reward, and not to shrink back in faithlessness.

Build Your House on the Rock of Christ

By wisdom a house is built, and through understanding it is established; through knowledge its rooms are filled with rare and beautiful treasures (**Prov. 24:3-4**).

Have you ever walked through a magnificent home designed by an accomplished interior designer? Everything is placed strategically to open the rooms and to provide comfort, beauty, and warmth. This is the picture of the "house of wisdom." You don't necessarily notice the details, but you sense the symmetry and loveliness of its design. The house of wisdom uses a unique design: the Word of God. It points to an eternal dwelling place filled with rare and beautiful treasures.

In 1 Corinthians 3:9-16, Paul calls the church in Corinth "God's building." Paul laid a foundation of the gospel message and someone else built on it. Different kinds of building materials are used: "gold, silver, costly stones, wood, hay and stubble." By the wise use of the better materials, a builder will fill the rooms of her house with rare and beautiful treasures: heavenly rewards. Otherwise, our work will be burned up when tested by the fire of Christ's judgment (2 Cor. 5:10).

The wise woman will build for the long term, and with the guidance of many counselors. Make sure you build on the only secure foundation: the Lord Jesus Christ. Then build with the best materials, using the building code of the ages, God's Word.

Scriptural Examples

The wise and foolish builders. Bob once built high-rise condominiums on Florida's coast. He drove pilings deep into the sand and anchored them to that solid rock. Nearby, other buildings did not use pilings. Some day a hurricane will move them across the street. Jesus gave two biblical examples of people who built their houses on the sand and on the rock. These builders had different results because of the different designs they used (Matt. 7:24-27).

Prayer of Application

Father, thank You for the Word of God, which gives us the guidance needed for the construction of our permanent dwelling and for trusting in Christ's foundation that is so firm and secure.

Store Up the Treasures of Christ

In the house of the wise are stores of choice food and oil, but a foolish man devours all he has. He who pursues righteousness and love finds life, prosperity, and honor (**Prov. 21:20-21**).

Jesus said, "Do not store up for yourselves treasures on earth" (Matt. 6:19). But here we see the wise man's house containing choice treasure, while the house of the foolish man contains nothing. How are we to resolve this apparent contradiction?

Jesus was not telling us to stop planning for the future. The prudent person will lay up a storehouse for future contingencies and needs. The difference lies in the placement of trust. The wise woman will recognize that God is the source of all material and spiritual blessings, and even though she wisely stores up for the future, she does not put trust in her earthly stores.

The foolish woman uses up her treasure through her appetites. She may be a drunkard, a shopaholic, or one who lives beyond her means. She is not prudent in her handling of money.

The real treasure of this life and the next is Jesus Christ. His is the righteousness and the love that we are to pursue with all of our heart, mind, and strength (Deut. 6:5; Luke 10:27). The rewards of His treasure house are mind-boggling and eternal (Matt. 6:20). Store up Christ's treasures.

Scriptural Examples

Ruth. She didn't have much of this world's treasures, but she pursued righteousness and love. She was blessed by God with the life, prosperity, and honor promised here (Ruth 3:10).

Job and Abraham. These were two of the richest men who ever lived. God delighted to honor them because of their faithfulness, righteousness, and kindness to others (Gen. 12:1; Job 1:1-3).

Paul. He pressed on in pursuit of the high goal toward which Christ had called him. Forgetting what was behind, he set his sights on an eternal prize (Phil. 3:12-14).

Prayer of Application

Lord, help me to be a good steward over all You have placed in my hands. May I trust only in Your sovereign power to sustain me and in the hope of Your treasures in heaven.

Exhibit the Riches You Have in Christ

One man pretends to be rich, yet has nothing; another pretends to be poor, yet has great wealth (**Prov. 13:7**).

In every city in America there is a section (or sections) of town that is known for its fancy houses and cars. There's also a lot of fancy indebtedness in places like that. Many people who live there are living on the hope of future earnings and really only pretending to be rich. Conversely, we sometimes hear of a person who lives like a hermit but is extremely wealthy. Hettie Green was such a woman who lived in New York some years ago. She appeared to be poor but died with a portfolio worth millions.

As Christians, we may be rich in this world's material goods, or we may be poor; but each of us has untold riches in Christ Jesus. Here again, however, deceit is often practiced. There are those who claim to know Christ and to be rich in eternal life, but are phonies and have nothing. Such people are like the Pharisees who sought God's favor through their "good works." Then we have Christians who are rich beyond measure in spiritual things, but who pretend to be poor, by being "closet" Christians. Jesus commands people like these to put their candle on top of a stand, not under a basket. By letting your riches in Christ be made apparent to all, you bring honor and glory to your Father in heaven (Matt. 5:15-16).

Scriptural Examples

The Gibeonites. These people pretended to be something they were not. They clothed themselves with rags and carried moldy bread, posing as people who had traveled a great distance. They were saved from certain death, but they served the Israelites as slaves from that time on (Josh. 9:3-27).

The Pharisees and scribes. These men wore long, flowing robes and were Israel's spiritual leaders during the time of Christ. They pretended to be righteous but Jesus condemned them, calling them "blind guides" and "hypocrites" (Matt. 23).

Prayer of Application

O Lord, You have made me rich in the things of Christ. Help me to reflect those riches in my life by the words that I speak, the actions that I take, and, yes, even in my every thought.

Seek the Rewards of Righteousness

*An evil man is trapped by his sinful talk, but a righteous man
escapes trouble. From the fruit of his lips a man is filled with good
things as surely as the work of his hands rewards him*
(**Prov. 12:13-14**).

A common theme in Proverbs is that of the justice and mercy
of God in rewards (see 13:21, for instance). Here we see the wicked
person sinning by her words, for which God will justly repay her;
possibly in this life, but certainly in the life to come (Matt. 12:36-
37). The righteous person may also transgress. But God rewards
her with merciful discipline and brings her out of trouble.

This righteous woman, justified before God only by the
atoning work of Christ, should seek to be satisfied by the fruit of
her lips (Prov. 13:2) and her hands. In other words, she should be
concerned only with the rightness of what she says and does, not
with what specific reward she will get for it. Jesus commands us
to seek those eternal rewards that do not vanish like the wind
(Matt. 6:19). Obediently seek the rewards of God.

Scriptural Examples

The Amalekite messenger. This man, apparently thinking
he'd be rewarded, ran to David in Ziklag to tell him of the deaths
of Saul and Jonathan in battle with his countrymen. As David
questioned him, he discovered that the messenger himself had
mortally wounded Saul. The messenger, trapped in his own words,
was struck and killed on orders from King David (2 Sam. 1:1-16).

Caleb and Joshua. These men urged the people to believe God
and go in and take the land. Caleb and Joshua were saved from
trouble by the fruit of their lips and were rewarded with entrance
into the Promised Land (Num. 14:6-10, 24).

Moses. He preferred to be mistreated with the people of God
rather than enjoy the treasures of Egypt, because he looked forward
to his reward (Heb. 11:24-28).

Prayer of Application

Heavenly Father, forgive me for not seeking reward from You
alone. Help me to trust You more, and not to set my heart on
earthly rewards but only those treasures in the life to come.

Accumulate Eternal Treasures

*The house of the righteous contains great treasure, but the income
of the wicked brings them trouble* (**Prov. 15:6**).

Although there is nothing inherently wrong with earthly
wealth, one should know the ground rules and pitfalls before
accumulating it. First, earthly wealth is an elusive treasure that
often takes wings and flies away. Second, earthly wealth can
become an idol, and the root cause of other sins (1 Tim. 6:10).
Third, earthly riches bring more accountability before God (Luke
12:48). Fourth, earthly riches can trouble one's household because of coveteousness, envy, and pride. Fifth, earthly riches never
seem to satisfy. The more you have, the more you need. Sixth, and
finally, there is no correlation between how hard you work and
how rich you will become. All wealth comes from God, and if He
doesn't want you to have it, you won't get it (Ps. 75:7).

On the other hand, the home filled with the riches of Christ
is infinitely wealthy. Our heavenly Father promises to meet all of
our needs through His riches in Christ Jesus (Phil. 4:19). These
vast and precious riches are in the house of the righteous: his heart.
They are eternal, and as such cannot be stolen or corrupted. And
they are only the down payment of the promised treasure of our
heavenly home; treasure infinitely superior to what a Rockefeller
or Trump could muster (1 Cor. 2:9).

Scriptural Examples

Abraham's riches. Abraham had immense wealth, but his
earthly walk was characterized by trusting God (Gen. 13:2).

Job's riches. Job was exceedingly rich, yet he did not set his
heart on his earthly treasure. Instead, Job's treasure was in knowing
the One who gave him the treasure (Job 1:3).

The man who found a treasure. Jesus likened the kingdom of
heaven to a treasure in a field, which, on finding it, a man sold all
that he had and bought that field (Matt. 13:44-46).

Prayer of Application

Lord, help me to see that Your eternal treasures are so much
more valuable than fickle earthly wealth. May I look only to You
for all my needs, as I look forward to my heavenly home.

Study Questions and Projects

1) Read Leviticus 25:18-19. What did God promise the Israelites if they would obey His commandments? Do we Christians have any such promise for this life? Think of the apostles and women of New Testament days. Did not their lives have more in common with Jesus' statement in John 16:33? Discuss with others.

2) What reward did Jesus promise the rich young ruler in Mark 10:21 if he would give his possessions to the poor?

3) Jesus promised an eternal reward for what situation in Luke 6:22 -23? What are we to do for an eternal reward in Luke 6:35 that is counter to this world's way of thinking?

4) In Hebrews 11:26, what does the writer say was Moses' motivation for following Christ? In 11:35, what motivated some persecuted saints of God to refuse to be released from prison?

5) In several places the Bible speaks of different crowns being given out as rewards in heaven. Of what crown do each of these verses speak, and for what is it given?

   a) 2 Timothy 4:8 - _____

   b) James 1:12 - _____

   c) 1 Peter 5:4 - _____

Other Verses to Study
Isaiah 40:10-11; Hebrews 12:1-2; Revelation 2:10; 22:12.

One to Memorize
By wisdom a house is built, and through understanding it is established; through knowledge its rooms are filled with rare and beautiful treasures (Prov. 24:3-4).

My Personal Action Plan to Be a Woman Who Is Rewarded

1) _____ 2) _____

3) _____ 4) _____

BIBLIOGRAPHY

Aitken, Kenneth T., *Proverbs*, The Westminster Press, Philadelphia, PA: 1986.

Alden, Robert L., *Proverbs: A Commentary on an Ancient Book of Timeless Advice*, Baker Book House, Grand Rapids, MI:1983.

Bridges, Charles, *A Commentary On Proverbs*, The Banner of Truth Trust, Carlisle, PA, First published: 1846.

Ironside, H.A., *Proverbs and the Song of Solomon*, Loizeaux Bros., Neptune, NJ, First published: 1908.

Kidner, Derek, *Proverbs: Tyndale Old Testament Commentaries*, D.J. Wiseman, General Editor, InterVarsity Press, Downer's Grove, IL: 1975.

Lawson, George, *Commentary On Proverbs*, Kregel Publications, Grand Rapids, MI, First Published: 1829.

McGee, J. Vernon, *Thru The Bible, Vol. 3*, Thru The Bible Radio, Pasadena, CA: 1982.

Nave, Orville J., *Nave's Topical Bible*, Baker Book House, Grand Rapids, MI: 1984.

Ross, Allen P., "Proverbs" section of *Expositor's Bible Commentary*. Frank E. Gaebelien, Gen Ed., Zondervan Publishing House, Grand Rapids, MI: 1991.